The Manifestations of Political Power Structures in Documentary Film

Media Production & Media Aesthetics

Edited by Kerstin Stutterheim and Martina Schuegraf

Volume 8

Zur Qualitätssicherung und Peer Review der vorliegenden Publikation

Die Qualität der in dieser Reihe erscheinenden Arbeiten wird vor der Publikation durch einen Herausgeber der Reihe geprüft.

Notes on the quality assurance and peer review of this publication

Prior to publication, the quality of the work published in this series is reviewed by one of the editors of the series.

Dror Dayan

The Manifestations of Political Power Structures in Documentary Film

PETER LANG

Bibliographic Information published by the Deutsche Nationalbibliothek
The Deutsche Nationalbibliothek lists this publication in the Deutsche Nationalbibliografie; detailed bibliographic data is available in the internet at http://dnb.d-nb.de.

Library of Congress Cataloging-in-Publication Data
A CIP catalog record for this book has been applied for at the Library of Congress.

ISSN 2365-2993
ISBN 978-3-631-80877-1 (Print)
E-ISBN 978-3-631-81452-9 (E-PDF)
E-ISBN 978-3-631-81453-6 (EPUB)
E-ISBN 978-3-631-81454-3 (MOBI)
DOI 10.3726/b16693

© Peter Lang GmbH
Internationaler Verlag der Wissenschaften
Berlin 2020
All rights reserved.

Peter Lang – Berlin · Bern · Bruxelles · New York · Oxford · Warszawa · Wien

All parts of this publication are protected by copyright. Any utilisation outside the strict limits of the copyright law, without the permission of the publisher, is forbidden and liable to prosecution. This applies in particular to reproductions, translations, microfilming, and storage and processing in electronic retrieval systems.

This publication has been peer reviewed.

www.peterlang.com

*Dedicated to all who try and change the world,
rather than merely film it.*

Preface: The smoking truck driver

"We had such a great shooting day, we managed to get a great close-up of a real typical Argentinian" said my classmate victoriously. We were sitting in a rented apartment in Buenos Aires, where we travelled as several student crews to shoot short films for a university project. "He was driving with one arm outside the truck's window, smoking, you know, like a typical Argentinian". I thought of Argentinian people I knew, such as my grandparents or my father, born and raised not far from where we sat, and couldn't remember a single time I saw any of them smoking, let alone with their hand outside the window of a moving truck. But by that time, it was already quite clear to me that in exchange programmes such as this one, which often tend to resemble expeditions more than exchanges, the students' presuppositions regarding class and race usually supersede the experienced reality. At least once a year my university would send students to produce films in other countries, mostly of the Global South, and I have noticed that the footage and films they brought back with them usually had little to do with the realities on the ground and much more to do with asserting their own views of the world. I attempted to raise the issue a few times during screenings and lectures, but quickly found that my syllabus as a cinematography student did not equip me with the proper critical and analytical tools to be able to formulate why the rushes or rough cuts on the screen seemed to me so racist or exploitative.

Only after finishing my diploma and starting my postgraduate programme, in which I directed and shot my first feature documentary, *Even Though My Land is Burning*, did this question become a critical issue for me. Born and raised an Israeli Jew in Jerusalem and filming a documentary in one of the hotspots of Palestinian popular resistance at the time, the village of Nabi Saleh, I knew I had a political responsibility to be much more critical regarding the way I present my protagonists than the way I was taught was acceptable. Realizing I am missing the tools for such critique, I started exploring the topic more closely, understanding that it raises questions which merit closer attention.

While the political power of images has been discussed as an issue ever since photography exists, it seems our times are seeing a rise in the way images and media become conveyors of ideology. Photos and videos play a major role in shaping public opinion in the West regarding ongoing conflicts in the Global South, with Syria, Venezuela, or Palestine being some clear examples. Countless documentaries on those topics are produced, streamed online and nominated for prestigious awards. The line between journalism, entertainment, and propaganda seems blurred than ever before, making it crucial to develop clear, palatable tools for the political readings of documentary film.

This book, and the doctoral thesis on which it is based, is an attempt to synthesize different theories and approaches I learned through practical filmmaking experience. It is a practice-based research, drawing concretely on two films I made and utilizing the knowledge gained while filming them: *Even Though My Land is Burning* (2016) and *Not Just Your Picture* (2019). One of the most important things I learned from my filmmaking – as well as from political work I took part in – is the importance of the dialectic of theory and practice, an understanding I strive to implement in this research.

In the following pages, I will introduce crucial theories for the reading of a documentary film for its political content. After a short overview of the state of the research today, I will present my methodological approaches of hermeneutics and dialectic and introduce key issues for the political understanding of documentary film. Some of those issues pertain to material conditions – film is an art form which often necessitates access to financial means, and as such, many canonical documentaries have had connection to capital or to elements of the ruling class as financers or commissioners. Other issues relate to the relationship between content and form and the importance of understanding it as part of an approach towards critically analysing a work of art.

The main part of the thesis is presented in Chapter 4, as I explore the way political power structures are manifested in different aesthetic means of the documentary or, in other words, how political content and cinematic form relate to each other. I will do this by introducing theories and approaches from different related fields and exploring their applications to case studies of existing documentaries as well as my own practical work. Unless stated otherwise, information regarding the films presented in the case studies is taken from the Internet Movie Database (IMDb.com). In order to help the reader in understanding the production context of the films discussed, I have opted for an in-text citation style for films which refers to director, country of production, and year.

Acknowledgements

This work would not have been possible without the support and confidence of so many colleagues, friends and political partners along the way. It will not be possible to list them all, but I do wish to thank Ben Ronen, the main protagonist of *Even Though My Land is Burning*, for his trust throughout the filming process, as well as Bassem Tamimi, Manal Tamimi, Oren Ziv, and all the other activists who appear in it. I am extremely thankful to all the friends and comrades in Germany, Palestine and around the world who have taught me so much, and especially to Layla and Ramsis Kilani, the main protagonists in *Not Just Your Picture*, as well as to its co-director Anne Paq, for allowing me with them on this journey.

From the Film University *Konrad Wolf* Babelsberg in Germany, I wish to thank Michael Hammon, Peter Badel and Stephan Krumbiegel for their help and guidance. In the Bournemouth University in the UK I wish to thank first and foremost my supervisor, professor Kerstin Stutterheim, who motivated me to take a leap of faith and come to Bournemouth, for her feedback, critical guidance, and immense support. I also wish to thank Candida Yates, my second supervisor, as well as James Fair and the teaching staff for all their help. A further thanks goes to Dan Laverick for proofreading my original dissertation.

This research as well as any of my films could never have been done without the love and support of my family, and I wish to thank Yael and Arie Dayan and Asal Akhavan for all they've done for me through the years and especially for all I've learned from them about living life as a critical, independent person.

Table of Contents

1. Understanding documentary as a political text: state of the research 17

2. Methodology and context 21
   2.1 Methodology 21
      Dialectical and historical materialism 21
      Hermeneutics 23
   2.2 Context 23
      Reflections on the political origins of documentary 23
      Power structures in documentary film 26
      The political dialectic of content and form in documentary film 29

3. The cinematic means as loci of power structures 35
   3.1 Social and political power structures in "Even Though My Land is Burning" and "Not Just Your Picture" 35
      "Even Though My Land is Burning" 36
      "Not Just Your Picture" 38
   3.2 Documentary characters: choice of protagonists as a political narrative 42
      The political dialectic of characters and society 44
          "Hoop Dreams" 48
          "Welcome to Leith" 53
      Individualism and the neo-liberal structure 57
          "King of Kong: A Fistful of Quarters" 59
          "Man on Wire" 61
          "Love Me" 62
      Characters and society in my practical work 65
      Conclusion 68
   3.3 Reflexivity and participatory film 69

"I'm harboring a murderer in my film" – Reflexivity and participation as content/form dialectic in the films of Avi Mograbi 74
    "Once I Entered a Garden" 75
    "Between Fences" 78
    "Z32" 81
"I am a refugee and a filmmaker, and you ask me to choose which?" – experiences of reflexivity and participation in my practical work 85
    "Even Though My Land is Burning" 86
    "Not Just Your Picture" 89
    "Limbo" 91

3.4 The power structures of the interview 95
    Historical emergence of the interview form 96
    Aesthetic and form of the interview 97
        Talking Head 97
        Vox Pop 98
        Conversation, dialogue or pseudo-dialogue 101
        The Masked Interview 101
    Theoretical approaches to different interview forms 102
        "The Fog of War" 104
    The power relations of interviews 105
    Interviews in my practical work 107

3.5 'You are looking at us like insects' – camera, sequence and the filmmaker´s gaze 109
    "Workingman´s Death" 112
        "Les Maîtres Fous" 115
        "Black Panthers" 117
    Politics of the gaze in my own practical work 120

4. Conclusion 127

Table of Contents 13

List of film stills 129

List of films 131

Bibliography 133

Abstract

The aim of this practice-led research is to explore the ways in which the political and social power structures between filmmaker and protagonist are manifested in the aesthetics and cinematic means of documentary film. Through a synthesis of filmmaking practice and "hidden knowledge" with critical theories from the fields of cultural studies and political philosophy the research devise methodological approaches to the critical analysis of documentary films in light of the political and material conditions of their emergence. By exploring filmmaking practice, both through the practical aspects of the research as well as through experiences made and reported by filmmakers, and placing those in the context of wider theories pertaining to issues of power structures and representation, it sheds light on the different aspects which must be considered when approaching the analysis of a documentary film for its ideological and political content.

The work also asserts that in order to fully understand and analyse a documentary film, a wider range of factors must be considered, most prominently the material conditions of the filmmaking process. Those include the financing and commissioning of the film, the conditions of its production as well as its distribution and reception. Drawing on methodologies of dialectical materialism in cultural studies, the research approaches the studied films as well as the practical experiences in a holistic fashion, contextualising them in historical, political and cultural processes instead of viewing them as isolated texts divorced from social context.

Keywords: Film Studies, Documentary Film, Dialectics, Hermeneutics

1. Understanding documentary as a political text: state of the research

Extensive scholarship and research have been conducted pertaining to the political aspects of documentary film and its reading as a political text, pointing to its inherent political character as a medium dealing with the real and the social. Chapter 3 of this book provides an overview of relevant literature and theories, which are further explored and applied throughout this thesis. Here it suffices to provide an account of the general literature used as well as literature which, however influential, was omitted from further references due to limitations of scope.

Beginning this research from the position of a practitioner with basic academic knowledge, I first studied the existing literature on documentary and turned to several well-established works as my starting point. Brian Winston's *Claiming the Real II: Grierson and Beyond* (2008) and Michael Chanan's *Politics of Documentary* (2007) have offered me a good first step in the understanding of the historical, social and political context of documentary, as well as an introduction to further literature and methods. Both books have also strengthened my view that documentary film cannot be properly read, certainly not in the political sense, without considering the context of its production.

In the last couple of decades, it is practically impossible to conduct theoretical research in the field of documentary without coming across the works of Bill Nichols, which I read extensively as well (1981, 1991, 2010). His by now canonical concept of the documentary modes has been eye-opening for me as a way to categorize and conceptualize the reading of documentaries, and has proven itself – as I made my first steps as a lecturer of documentary film – to be an invaluable framework for the theorization of documentary for students. The further I advanced with my research, however, the more I came to the understanding that although Nichols' work is highly relevant to my work – his understanding of the interview as a locus of power structures being one clear example – some of his theories, primarily his "modes of documentary", offer an excessively rigid structure often inapplicable to many modern documentaries or to the experiences I myself have accrued as a practitioner. In the chapter of this book dealing with participation and reflexivity I attempt to clarify why Nichols' modes are better considered as different spectrums of cinematic approaches than categories. This view of Nichols' modes is shared by other scholars, such as Stella Bruzzi, who sees them as 'crude' and 'breathtakingly simplistic', imposing a 'false chronology onto what is essentially a theoretical paradigm' and 'necessarily circumscribed by his own preferences and areas of knowledge' (2006, p. 3–4). While I subscribe to Bruzzi's criticism, Nichols' approach is still a necessary step in my own understanding of the academic discourse, and is a necessary stepping stone for documentary theory, if only for its by now hegemonic status in the field.

The experiences I gathered through my political work in the years leading up to my research have introduced me to Marxist thinking and epistemology, and the applications of Marxist theories to cultural and film studies proved themself useful for my research as well. There, the writings of Mike Wayne have proven highly instructive and have shown me how such theories can be and are integrated in the field of film studies (cf. 2001, 2003, 2005). Wayne's work has also pointed me in the direction of the literary critique of Hungarian Marxist philosopher Georg Lukács, whose influence is present in some parts of this paper (cf. 1970, 1979). Those writings led to my integration of dialectical-materialist approaches into my methodology and has thoroughly shaped my research and understanding of the subject matter. The economical and political crisis of the last decade have sparked a resurgence of interest in Marxism and the applicability of its ideas and methods (cf. Jeffries 2012), among the left as well as the right,[1] and this research has proven to me that such methods are highly valuable in the field of cultural studies. In order to better understand such and similar approaches, I turned to the works of intellectuals from the field of critical theory as well, such as Theodor W. Adorno (1958) and Raymond Williams (2005). While I do not refer to Williams directly in this work, both have proven invaluable to further my understanding of dialectics and historical and dialectical materialism in the context of culture and art.

Since the focus of my work is power relations in documentary films, acquiring an understanding of the definition of power was necessary. I have consulted several works in sociology, such as the writings of Pierre Bourdieu (cf. 2005) or Michel Foucault (cf. 1991), but have found them less applicable to the specifics of my work. The definition of power in documentary work is an intricate one which can be approached from different directions: for example, power can be seen as an issue of representation, such as in the works of British sociologist Stuart Hall (in Jhally 1997) or of Palestinian literature scholar Edward Said (2003), both

---

1 Marxist ideas and thinkers also seem to cause rising antagonism under the right, as demonstrated by the Budapest city council's decision to remove a statue of Georg Lukács from a public park in the city in 2017, or by the repeating vandalization of Karl Marx's grave in the Highgate cemetery in London in 2019.

discussed in Chapter 3. For this research, however, it was important for me to find a definition of power and power structures which will allow me to better examine the relations between the film and society, with society being intrinsically connected to its material conditions, and so it was sociologist Bob Jessop's work (2012) which allowed for important nuances for a relevant Marxist definition of power, discussed in Chapter 3.

In order to situate my work properly in the state of the research today, it is important to review works which I have consulted but are not referred to in this paper. Certainly, one of the works which influenced my perspective at the start of the research but ultimately did not play a critical role in shaping the finished work is *Transcultural Cinema* by anthropologist and filmmaker David MacDougall (1998). As someone coming from the world of fiction film and "standard" documentary, I was unfamiliar with the different political issues that are important for any critical visual anthropologist. MacDougall's work into ethnographic film and issues of participatory filmmaking has given me valuable tools to further reflect on the power discrepancies involved in documentary film.

Another interesting and relevant work in the field of visual anthropology is Ariella Azoulay's, whose works have been extremely constructive in forming an understanding of the politics of the image, especially since her main subject matter – Zionism and the occupation of Palestine – is also the focus of most of my practical works. Although she is not cited in this paper, her theories on photography being a set of encounters between the camera, the photographer and the subject on the one hand, and the photograph and the viewer on the other, thus formulating photography as a continuous event rather than a singular occurrence (cf. 2008), have helped me to understand the importance of viewing documentary film dialectically in the context of its creation as well as its reception. Her understanding of photography as a potential tool for acting in practical solidarity with the oppressed (cf. 2015) corresponds with the aims of my practical work, as detailed in Chapter 4.

It is also important to note that I decided to limit my research to documentary films which could be categorized as "theatrical" or "cinematic", excluding factual TV formats such as the reality show, the docu-soap or the docu-drama. Besides the considerations of scope, I have done this for two reasons: first, that I believe that with all the different cross-formats existing today, those media still often rely on different aesthetics and methods of production than film; second, since I see issues of commodification and commercial considerations as playing an even greater role in the field of TV formats than in that of documentary film, those issues would necessarily have shifted my research into different spheres. An example of a dialectical-materialist analysis of such a format can be found in Wayne's case study of *Big Brother* (2003). I did, however, include at times documentaries made for TV, such as *Class Divide* (Marc Levin, US 2015), since they are formally and aesthetically close enough to theatrical films to be relevant to the research. I also referred to an online video report by the German magazine *Die Welt* to exemplify a specific point which is relevant to documentary film, despite it lying outside the parameters of the stated subject matter of this research.

Another discussion intentionally left out regards the broader questions of objectivity and authenticity in documentary film. While an important topic, and one which is certainly relevant to the questions of political content of documentary, I decided that it exceeds the scope of this book and have mostly left out the works of scholars dealing with those questions such as Stella Bruzzi (2006). I do believe, however, that by showing the different ways in which a documentary is political, my position regarding the impossibility of a truly objective film will also be made clear.

Another important point to stress is that my research, although utilizing methods of historical materialism, does not itself constitute historical research. There are therefore several important film-historical works not directly discussed in this paper, such as *Documentary, a History of Non-Fiction Film* by Erik Barnouw (1974). *Documenting the Documentary* (Grant and Sloniowski 1998) is another example of a book touching on similar themes, mainly through case studies, which was excluded in order to maintain focus on newer documentaries where possible.

I also choose to concentrate the research on my own culture and to focus mainly on "White" European, US-American or Jewish-Israeli documentaries and filmmakers. This was done in order to fully draw upon my own position and subjective experiences as practitioner on the one hand, as well as to limit the research's scope to the specific issues of power structures of such films on the other. This choice has led to several important regions and tendencies being left out to a greater or lesser extent, most prominently films of the Global South and Soviet film. While I do address the films of such filmmakers as Dziga Vertov, his theoretical contribution to the understanding of documentary was mostly left out. I believe that Vertov's work, as a theoretician and practitioner who constantly sought out the interrelation between film and dialectical materialism, as well as Soviet film in general such as in the works of Esfir Shub or Sergei Eisenstein, merits a separate discussion which would go beyond the scope of this thesis. The same goes for other scholars concentrating on other non-Western films as well.

2. Methodology and context

2.1 Methodology

One of the main aims of my research is to argue and exemplify the intricate interrelations between documentary film and social and political conditions. I assert that the only way to properly analyse documentary film for its political substance is by avoiding the view of film as an individual text divorced from its surroundings. In my research, I will argue for a dialectic understanding of film, society and politics, and that any methodology for such research must involve a synthesis of different approaches which allows for a holistic and dialectic view of the subject matter, taking different elements and factors into consideration and concerning itself with the relationships between them.

Since this work necessarily deals to a large extent with the relationship between the concrete (the film) and the abstract (the social and political), so must its methodology, which might carry with it the risk of appearing unfocused at times. It must include approaches of dealing with the specific and concrete films in question, with their more general and abstract political conditions of production, as well as with the relations between the two. I therefore utilize two main approaches and attempt to interweave them into a methodology suitable to such an undertaking: one is the critical analysis of films, applying various theoretical approaches unto case studies, and the other is reflection upon my own practical work, using my "hidden knowledge" as a practitioner in order to theorize them. The term "hidden knowledge", primed at the CILECT meeting on "artistic research at film schools" in Paris in 2013, refers to theoretical knowledge gleaned through filmmaking practice. This is an important and valuable part of documentary scholarship, and I see its incorporation into theoretical analysis as paramount to my research. Films are made "on set", in real life, and cannot be analysed thoroughly from a purely theoretical, interpretative academic viewpoint (cf. Eco 1990). The challenges and material conditions of making the film must be acknowledged as well. My practical work discussed in this thesis, although carried out first and foremost as "regular" documentaries rather than academic research, is therefore part of the academic process of enquiry based on the dialectic of theory and practice on which I base my research.

Dialectical and historical materialism

In order to be able to properly locate the films in their political context, I draw on approaches of dialectical and historical materialism. As is demonstrated in the later chapters, this approach is particularly beneficial for the understanding of developments in the medium of documentary film and is not uncommon in the field of documentary film studies, although it is not always named or recognized as such. In simple terms, a methodology of dialectical materialism searches first and foremost for the material relations between elements, and for the way in which material contradictions and tensions bring about changes. It is therefore highly valuable in order to understand, for example, the interconnections between technological developments, financial conditions and new aesthetical approaches in film. This will be exemplified in greater detail in the next chapter.

A philosophy of dialectics was prominently developed by G.W.F. Hegel (cf. 1977) and reformulated by Karl Marx (cf. 1959, 1969) into what Marx termed dialectical materialism, whereby material conditions take precedence over ideas/the phenomenological rather than the reverse. Historical materialism is the application of this methodological approach to historical and social processes. For this reason, those two methods might overlap throughout this book: since I will often attempt to look at aspects of film in their film-historical perspective, the approach might be more of historical materialism, while the reading of films in the context of their specific and concrete material conditions of production might draw more on approaches of dialectical materialism. Since the two are, anyway, not separate approaches but rather the application of one to a more specific field, not much can be gained in this context by sharply distinguishing between them and I at times use them interchangeably. What is central to this thesis is an appreciation of dialectical analysis as a means of shedding light upon different material conditions, broadly considered, in their interrelationships with the film and each other, and bringing into focus the nature of material conditions as ever-changing in and through their relation to each other.

A first step towards understanding dialectic thinking can be made through Theodor W. Adorno's understanding of dialectic as 'always correcting itself' (1958, p. 10). Adorno defines dialectic as 'a way of thinking which does not make do with the conceptual order of things, but rather accomplishes the feat of correcting the conceptual order through the being of the things' (ibid.).[2] Bertell Ollman claims that

> Dialectics is a way of thinking that brings into focus the full range of changes and interactions that occur in the world. As part of this, it includes how to organize a reality

---

2   'Dialektik ist ein Denken, das sich nicht bei der begrifflichen Ordnung bescheidet, sondern die Kunst vollbringt, die begriffliche Ordnung durch das Sein der Gegenstände zu korrigieren.' (Translation mine)

viewed in this manner for purposes of study and how to present the results of what one finds to others, most of whom do not think dialectically. (2003, p. 12)

Hermeneutics

Although dialectical materialism offers an effective tool for a political reading of film history and the emergence of hegemonic approaches or for the locating of films in a socio-political context, alone and in itself it is also limited in its possibilities as a method to critically analyse a creative work. In order to thoroughly analyse a film for its political content it is therefore crucial to turn to other methods which concentrate on reading film as a text, being able to focus both on its particular aspects as well as on a reading of the whole (cf. Gillard 2009). For this reason, I will be utilizing hermeneutics in approaching the analysis of the different films discussed.

Some key hermeneutical concepts for my research are ones that deal with the relation between the parts and the whole of the text and between the text and its reader, such as the concept of the *hermeneutic circle* (cf. Gadamer 2010), suggesting a text be read through looking at those relations between the parts and the whole, as well as the general context in which the text is situated. Much like dialectical materialism, hermeneutics takes into consideration the text's relationship to outstanding elements, as it attempts to read texts in light of historical, social or cultural surroundings.

Part of a hermeneutic methodology is also the *symptomatic reading* (Koutsourakis 2015), a reading looking for that which is left out and supressed. This approach is also valuable for exposing the underlying ideological aspects of film, and has been used in the critical analysis of political film since the 1970s.

Using aspects of both those methodologies in tandem, hermeneutics and dialectical materialism, this paper approaches the analysis of the films discussed, as well as my own practical work, in a way which elucidates the intricate connections between film and ideology, between the production process and the political and social conditions surrounding it, without neglecting the critical analysis of film as a work of art and a text.

2.2 Context

Reflections on the political origins of documentary

Film is perhaps the art form most reliant upon – as well as initiating of – technological progress (Piccirillo 2011, par 1 sec 1). Its entire development and coming into being can be seen as a chain of advances in the fields of chemistry, electricity, optics, and physics, and significant moments in the history of film – fiction as well as documentary – can in most cases be attributed to innovations and discoveries resulting in new film equipment which allowed for more ambitious approaches and for new solutions to technical problems, all those in turn having immense effects on the medium's aesthetic potential.

Film's inherent reliance on equipment, technological innovation and at times cumbersome logistics have also meant that it is a medium for which financing plays a determining role. Although technological progress has led not only to new cinematic possibilities but also to a decrease in costs and an increase in the availability of equipment, producing documentaries still necessitates access to capital. As such, any materialist analysis of the origin of documentary must take into consideration early film's sources of finance and, of course, the influence and effect that those forces had on the medium and how this influence helped to shape canonical works and our understanding of documentary today. Although documentary is in most cases cheaper to produce than fiction film, the acquiring of financing through producers, commissioners or distributors plays a major role and is a determining factor in the production of documentaries.

Such a reading of the history of documentary film provides the framework for this research. Winston (2008, p. 24) analyses how Flaherty's *Nanook of the North* (USA 1922), considered one of the most influential films from the first decades of documentaries, cannot be understood without acknowledging the imperial and colonial context of its filming, and how this view is manifested in the different scenes. One example is the scene in which Nanook bites a record, a scene presenting him as primitive despite Allakariallak, playing Nanook, being well aware of what a record actually was but was using his mouth due to the severe cold (ibid.). It was much because the expansionist interests of the colonial forces at the time were served by presenting indigenous populations as weak and "backwards" that such a film was able to get the required funding, access and logistical support.

An even more telling example would be Arthur Elton and Edgar Astney's *Housing Problems* (UK 1935), which shows the intricate interplay between film, technology, capital and social conditions in shaping the ideological content as well as the aesthetics of documentary film. For *Housing Problems*, The British Commercial Gas Association contributed the financing needed to bring cutting edge film technology into the heart of one of the UK's most evident social troubles at the time – the run-down houses of its industrial proletariat. This material support allowed the filmmakers to conduct sync-sound interviews on location, making *Housing Problems* the first British documentary to utilise an aesthetic that would go on to become one of the main pillars of documentary film.

Accepting such a commission from the Commercial Gas Association meant accepting its commercial and ideological aims as well – to propagate for a demolition of entire neighbourhoods and to replace them with gas-heated buildings. It remains to be asked what would become of the interviewed workers featured in the film and whether such a measure would also be in their own interest: today such measures of "urban renewal" are often considered in the context of gentrification, displacement and social inequality. Indeed, Winston quotes Dutch filmmaker Joris Ivens commenting on the film: 'If the British films could have been sponsored directly by social organisations fighting the bad housing conditions, instead of by a gas company, they would have closed in on such dramatic reality as rent strikes and protest movements' (ibid., p. 64). While Ivens' critique might be harsh considering that the film – unlike many other GPO films – does in fact show the reality of working-class life in quite a radical way, *Housing Problems* is indeed a stark example of the inevitable connection between documentary film and capital, often resulting in film being a conveyer of ideology in the service of the latter, as well of the complexity of reading and analysing a documentary's political content.

These material connections between film and capital are mostly due to film's character as an art form and its reliance on the means of production which under capitalist conditions are unavailable to most. This reliance has, of course, a flipside to it: in situations in which the means of production are not controlled by capital, film will naturally become more accessible to other classes and can serve as a conveyer of other ideologies. Here the clearest example would be Soviet film, being the bearer of revolutionary or socialist ideology through the access to means of production given to it by the state. A historical example for such a case would be Lenin's dictate on the importance of film as propaganda and as means of reaching out to illiterate people in post-revolution Russia (Lenin 1934, p. 388–389).

It is for those reasons that a historical-materialist analysis is paramount for the political reading of documentary film – it shows us the underlying ideological currents which are crucial for the understanding of the film's context. This of course is not meant to propagate an approach of economic reductionism to film analysis: film is, inherently through its medial characteristics and despite (or perhaps also through) its commodification, an art form. But it is indeed an art form heavily based on material means, and as such will always maintain a certain connection to the class with the readiest access to them, a connection which will manifest itself in its aesthetics and content. Marx and Engels claim that 'The ideas of the ruling class are in every epoch the ruling ideas [...] The class which has the means of material production at its disposal, has control at the same time over the means of mental production' (1969, p. 47). As such, film, media and communication must be seen as playing a major role in the way society understands ideas and even constructs its collective cultural memory. Jan Assman proclaims that 'Memories, even personal, only emerge through the communication and interaction of social groups. We remember not only what we experience from others, but what has been told to us, confirmed as important and mirrored to us by others as well' (1999, p. 36).[3]

Power structures in documentary film

In order to approach the analysis of the aesthetic manifestations of power structures in documentary aimed for in this research, one must first come to a definition of power structures in film. Some common approaches to the question of power can be found in such works as those of Pierre Bourdieu (cf. 2005) and Michel Foucault (cf. 1991). In the arts and media studies, the question of power is often discussed in the context of representation and power of definition. Stuart Hall claims that

> the question of the circulation of meaning almost immediately involves the question of power. *Who* has the power, in *what* channels, to circulate *which* meanings to *whom*? Which is why the issue of power can never be bracketed out from the question of representation. (in Jhally 1997, p. 6)

In the context of documentary film, Hall's question of who is circulating which meaning can be seen as a question of authorial voice, of who speaks. American anthropologist Jay Ruby notes that 'Questions of voice, authority, and authorship have become a serious concern among documentary filmmakers ... Who can represent someone else ... [and] with what intention ... is a conundrum' (1991, p. 49). Ruby sees authorial voice as a form of power, and sharing or giving it up as having 'social, political and epistemological implications' (ibid.).

While in agreement with Hall and Ruby, I would add that issues of representation and voice, which pertain mainly to power in the discursive sense, are themselves only symptoms of material power, albeit crucial ones. In order to formulate a working definition of power structures in film for this research, one which identifies material conditions as ontologically prior to discourse, one must consider that in film, just as in society, power lies in the hands of those who own

---

3 'Erinnerungen auch persönlichster Art entstehen nur durch Kommunikation und Interaktion im Rahmen sozialer Gruppen. Wir erinnern nicht nur, was wir von anderen erfahren, sondern auch, was uns andere erzählen und was uns von anderen als bedeutsam bestätigt und zurückgespiegelt wird' (translation mine)

the means of production. This means that power structures and power relations are a question of exploitation as well. This exploitation can be direct, as when a filmmaker profits from the filming of her protagonists which themselves do not share the profit,[4] or it can be indirect, as in the case of *Nanook of the North* mentioned above, justifying or propagating material exploitation relevant to the film's subject matter.

I therefore suggest considering three aspects when defining power structures in documentary: first, who is exploiting or being exploited – either directly or indirectly. Second, who controls the means of production, and third, what are the overall material circumstances and context of the film's production.

One scholar whose work attempts to explore exploitation through art, media, and discourse is Edward Said, most prominently with his book *Orientalism* (1978). Although oft considered to be a work dealing mostly with the discursive representation of the Orient by the West, Gerald Sim, making the case for Said's crucial contribution to film studies (2012), argues for a Marxist reading of *Orientalism*, asserting that Said's work is definitely one dealing with the material conditions of the exploitation of the Orient, namely with respect to colonialism and imperialism:

> When he speaks of "power" in the book, he does not merely refer to an imbalance of cultural or social capital tilting in their *(UK, France and US)* favour; instead, power comes specifically from material expressions of imperialism [...] "The *strength* of Western cultural discourse" that he describes is not something ephemeral, intangible or figurative, but instead is the part of colonialism that materially and physically oppresses. (ibid., p. 241, parenthesis mine)

I will argue that this understanding of power is key for the reading of film, and will suggest that, just as in Winston's reading of *Nanook of the North* as an imperial work mentioned above, an anchoring of the film in the material context of its origination is crucial as one of the first steps towards developing an understanding of the power structures manifested in its aesthetic. To examine the first of the three aspects mentioned above, such an approach would claim that the exploited in such cases is not merely "the Orient" as a discursive construct, but rather the orient(al) as a colonial object.

---

4 The political economy of film as an industry, whether in documentary or fiction, and of cultural production and creative labour in general, is a highly relevant and important subject, but unfortunately one which will go beyond the scope of this research. For further reading, I recommend Mike Wayne's work on Marxism and media (cf. 2003).

Another early example of the direct and material connection between film and colonial exploitation can be seen in Basil Wright's *The Song of Ceylon*, a film which 'totally avoids the question of colonial labour and the economic exploitation of the colonies – which is not surprising, since it was produced by the GPO Film Unit in conjunction with the Ceylon Tea Propaganda Board' (Hood 1983, p. 102). Hood also points to the Empire Marketing Board, which appointed John Grierson as head of their film unit in 1928, whose aim 'was to promote the consumption of the products of the Empire as part of the attempt to make the Empire function as a self-sufficient economic system' (ibid., p. 101). While *Song of Ceylon* can and should be studied for its aesthetic merits, as well as for its depiction of the oriental Other, such examination should be conducted while critically reflecting on the fact that the film's production and commissioning were meant to serve the imperial interests of the time.

Of course, the coin of colonial film has a flipside: indigenous filmmaking has been constantly gaining ground in the last decades, and films in which indigenous people represent themselves rather than being represented must be considered as well (cf. Ginsburg 1991). Due to limitations of scope, this paper focuses more on "Western" documentaries, but theoretical frameworks such as Maori/New-Zealander filmmaker Barry Barclay's concept of "Fourth Cinema" (cf. 2003) or documentaries such as Palestinian filmmaker and activist Emad Burnat's *Five Broken Cameras* (with Guy Davidi, Palestine/Israel 2011) must be mentioned here as well.

In the narrow sense, the second of the three aspects of power structures I suggest considering, control of the means of production, could be analysed quite easily – it is in most cases the producer or the filmmaker who controls them. But in order to thoroughly understand the power structures in question one must attempt a broader view of the definition of power. Sociologist Bob Jessop notes that a Marxist approach to defining power often concerns itself with 'power relations as manifestations of a specific mode or configuration of class domination rather than as a purely interpersonal phenomenon lacking deeper foundations in the social structure' (2012, p. 3). It is crucial to not skew our understanding of power by focusing solely on the personal power relations between an individual filmmaker and protagonist, but to acknowledge the totality of social conditions which lies behind it. In Chapter 4.2 I will turn to the critical theories of Georg Lukács, who developed approaches for literature studies based on such perspectives (cf. 1970). But another key term helpful for this understanding might be Antonio Gramsci's studies of hegemony and the political role of intellectuals.

Gramsci saw hegemony as a way in which the consent of dominated groups is manufactured by the ruling class through political and intellectual means (cf. 1971). In this way, the interests of the ruling class are made to seem broader than they are and are reflected in the intellectual work of a society. Gramsci's analysis is highly important for a dialectical understanding of the politics of film, since it prevents a reductionist view according to which the power structures in film start and end with the entity signing off the budget or owning the cameras.

The third aspect I suggest considering is the overall material and historical circumstances of the film's production as well as its context. These can provide further insights into the economic and political interests of the involved parties as well as conditions pertaining to the film's reception. For example, in reflecting upon the commissioning of *Housing Problems* by a gas industry concerned that the rise of electric heating in London might damage their business (Hood 1983, p. 102), we establish a different reading of the film's structure and message, and in turn of its pioneering use of new aesthetic and technological innovations.

The aim here is therefore to study and establish the dialectical relationships between the film and the context of its origination, since I argue that those are inseparable from its aesthetics. I believe that the role that those conditions play in the decisions made by the filmmakers – consciously or unconsciously, by chance or by design – is crucial and too often overlooked. Documentary fundamentally deals with "the real". Since the real is always multi-faceted and rarely purely causal or linear, so should be our approach to the understanding of documentary film.

The political dialectic of content and form in documentary film

The attempt to understand the manifestations of the political in the documentary is presupposed by, in many ways even akin to, the understanding of the relationship between the film's content and form. In many currents in film studies, this relationship is presented as a simple duality in which the content pertains to the subject matter while the form to the style or cinematic means (cf. Mooney 2015). This conception of the dichotomy, however, does not help us to understand the intricate relationship between (political) content and form, a relationship which I argue should be understood in two ways. First, artistically, as an inseparable dialectical unity necessary for art to perform its social and aesthetic tasks (cf. Lukács 1970). Second, in the more general epistemological meaning used, for example, in Hegelian philosophy: in terms of the contradictions between a thing's *appearance* and its *being*, between what it is and what it claims or is perceived to be (cf. Adorno 1958). I argue that those two understandings of film (which are themselves not separate but rather two sides of the same dialectic approach) are crucial, and that the best way to utilize them is through hermeneutics and dialectical methods as explained above.

Georg Lukács, whose work I will refer to in more detail in Chapter 4.2, takes his point of departure in Hegel's abstract definition that 'content is nothing but the conversion of form into content, and form is nothing but the conversion of content into form' (quoted in Lukács 1970, p. 45). Lukács builds on that definition to arrive at the conclusion that the question of content and form presents a question of artistic epistemology and objectivity. He sees art as similar to science in the sense that its goal is to transcend the contradictions between appearance and being, between universal and particular, and so to establish artistic integrity as that which is objective and, as much as possible, true – much like science strives to make the imperceptible perceptible in order to understand natural phenomena. According to Lukács, since the content of a work of art necessarily 'provides a greater or lesser extract of reality' (ibid., p. 47), it is the role of the form to provide context so as to make this extract not appear as a mere extract but as a 'self-contained whole' (ibid.), thus legitimizing its truth claim.

Furthermore, Lukács notes that it is devices of form such as the plot which allow for 'the dialectic of human existence and consciousness (to) be expressed' (ibid., p. 51), since they situate the characters in such a relation to their social environment, that they are given cause to take certain actions which demonstrate to the reader the contrast and contradictions between what those characters appear to be and what they really are. This is a good example of how the two understandings of the content-form dialectic described above work together in critique: it is through the dialectic of content (here, characters) and form (here, plot) that an artistic truth about the characters is revealed, by addressing their own inherent dialectic of "content" (what they objectively are) and "form" (what they appear to be).

Antonio Gramsci asserts that the fact that content and form present a unity does not mean that they cannot be discussed separately (1985, p. 203), although it might be "easier" to discuss content than form since content can often be analysed and summarized in more logical or concrete ways (ibid.). A further point made by Gramsci is especially useful for the analysis of film – that a work of art is a process, and that what one may see as changes in content are also changes in form: 'The first content that was unsatisfactory was also form and, in reality, when one arrives at a satisfying 'form', the content has also changed' (ibid.). This is an experience one can certainly derive from the process of editing a film as well.

David Leopold notes that for Gramsci, whose political work deals predominantly with questions of cultural and political hegemony, the content/form question can also be applied to society itself, with the content relating to the material forces, the economic base, and the form to ideology (2013, p. 30). This is analogous to the aim of this research: to find the ways in which the material is manifested in the immaterial, and to unravel the underlying power structures and relationships of seemingly independent and autonomous ideas.

While this kind of work, which has been mostly conducted in the field of literature provides us with useful concepts and approaches for the political analysis of documentary, in certain aspects it can only take us so far. There are key elements in film – and in documentary especially –which differ immensely from literature, such as, for example, questions of technique, of imitation of reality, and, as mentioned before, of the sheer material and financial cost and effort needed for the production of a film. Film is also a time-based art form, and as such its reception is quite different to that of literature, wherein the reader is able to pause, repeat, and reflect at her own pace, in contrast to the way films are usually watched.

It is therefore important to turn to experiences of practicing filmmakers when discussing an understanding of content and form. One such work by a practitioner and theoretician is the essay *for an imperfect cinema* by Cuban director Julio García Espinosa (1979), who sees a correlation between "perfect" and "reactionary" cinema. Espinosa's essay is important since it directly connects the question of the "perfectness" of form with the unequal distribution of the means of film production, which are (and at the time of the essay's writing much more so than today) only accessible to an elite few. For Espinosa, imperfect cinema is only interested in one thing: the way in which the artist overcomes the elitist conventions which condition and determine the form (ibid., p. 26). This also relates to the artist's commitment and involvement:

> A new poetics for the cinema will, above all, be a "partisan" and "committed" poetics, a "committed" art, a consciously and resolutely "committed" cinema — that is to say, an "imperfect" cinema. An "impartial" or "uncommitted" (cinema), as a complete aesthetic activity, will only be possible when it is the people who make art. (p. 25)

In this way, Espinosa poses an important question, one which is worth re-examining today in light of the immense changes in the accessibility of film equipment: whether a "perfect" or "imperfect" cinematic form indicates a certain social or political content. Espinosa, however, is also not suggesting a dichotomist correlation between a perfect/imperfect form and a revolutionary/reactionary content. He is rather arguing that as long as film production remains the realm of the elite few, as long as film – and more importantly, the whole of society – is not truly democratized, the 'perfect' cinema will always remain a privilege and a tool of the exploiting class. Mike Wayne explains in a way which also sheds light on the often-discussed issue of objectivity in documentary film:

> An 'impartial' art is premature in a world full of 'partialities' (social, economic and cultural inequalities). [...] When it is the people who make art, art will no longer be caught up in sectional interests. [...] The key point though is that we do not live in such a world today and so art cannot be divorced from the conflictual social interests which are at play. (2001, p. 13)

Argentinian filmmakers Octavio Getino and Fernando Solanas describe this relationship between the aesthetic and the ideological through a historical-materialist analysis of the means and technologies of film production:

> The placing of the cinema within US models, even in the formal aspect, in language, leads to the adoption of the ideological forms that gave rise to precisely that language and no other. Even the appropriation of models which appear to be only technical, industrial, scientific, etc. leads to a conceptual dependency situation... The 35mm. camera, 24 frames a second, arc lights, and a commercial place of exhibition for audiences were conceived not to gratuitously transmit any ideology, but to satisfy ... the cultural and surplus value needs of a specific ideology... that of US financial capital ... a cinema conceived as a show to be exhibited in large theaters with a standard duration, hermetic structures that are born and die on the screen ... leads to the absorption of forms of the bourgeois world-view which are the continuation of 19th century art, of bourgeois art: man is accepted only as a passive and consuming object. (1969, p. 119–120)[5]

As Getino and Solanas note, the political dialectic of content and form cannot be studied and understood without taking into consideration the reception of the work by the audience and the further dialectical relation coming into play through screening and viewing. Cuban filmmaker Tomás Gutiérrez Alea notes that:

> it's only a simplistic solution to consider form and content as two separate ingredients [...] Furthermore, this attitude considers the spectator as a passive entity [...] It does not have anything to do with a dialectical understanding of the process of an organic integration of form and content, in which both aspects are seen to be indissolubly united at the same time that they work off of and interpenetrate each other, even to the point where they take over each other's functions in that reciprocal interplay [...] The diverse modalities of their mutual interaction [...] give rise to various levels of "productivity" [...] in the work's relation to the spectator. (1984, p. 9)

---

5 Such analysis becomes even more crucial when one considers the amount of Hollywood films created with assistance from the Pentagon since WWII, as published through an FOIA request by Dr. Stephen Underhill of the Marshall University in the US (Underhill 2013).

Brian Winston points to the role the conditions of viewing the film play in analysing it:

> It is, for instance, one thing for a direct cinema film-maker in America to claim, on no ground whatsoever, that the audience has a new relationship to the screen when viewing his work; it is quite another for Fernando Solanas and Octavio Getino to make a similar claim for members of their audience[6] [...] not least because such attendance was illegal and subject to extreme repression [...] That is scarcely the situation for a person choosing to watch a direct cinema programme transmitted on an American public television station, or a Michael Moore movie in a local mall cinema. (2008, p. 284)

The audience and the way it receives the film therefore play an important role in the analysis of the political dialectic of content and form in documentary, one which must be considered as well.

---

6   Winston is referring to Solanas and Getino's *Hour of the Furnaces* (Argentina 1968).

3. The cinematic means as loci of power structures

This chapter will examine the way power structures between filmmaker and protagonists and the political content of a documentary are manifested in its aesthetic and various cinematic means. Due to considerations of scope it will concentrate on the most relevant aspects, which will be introduced through the lens of different theories, case studies and experiences from my own practical work.

It begins with a short overview of my own films that are referred to in this thesis, focusing on the power relations that exist between myself and the protagonists and the films' political and cinematic handling of their subject matter.

3.1 Social and political power structures in "Even Though My Land is Burning" and "Not Just Your Picture"

The practical part of my research entails documentary work I have conducted in the years following up to the research. Those are the feature documentaries *Even Though My Land is Burning* (2016) and *Not Just Your Picture* (2019). Both films present certain challenges and problems pertaining to the power structures between filmmaker and protagonists, as they both deal with the topic of the Israeli occupation of Palestine, an issue I am directly involved in as a filmmaker, being a Jewish-Israeli citizen enjoying certain privileges while filming. One of many examples of such privileges is the fact that Israelis and Palestinians are subjected to different court systems in certain parts of Palestine, as well as to different treatment by the military and police (cf. Yehuda et al. 2014), presenting different physical and judicial risks to me compared to those faced by some of my protagonists while filming.

Even Though My Land is Burning was produced as a no-budget project by me and had its premiere in Berlin in March 2016. *Not Just Your Picture* is a co-directed project, an element that will also be addressed, produced together with the French photojournalist Anne Paq, who at the time was already working on her web-documentary *Obliterated Families* (Paq and Qandil 2016), documenting the stories of families who had lost three or more members in the 2014 Israeli attacks on Gaza. One of the stories was that of the Kilani family, who became the protagonists of *Not Just Your Picture*.

Our work on the feature was organised in a non-hierarchical way, with both of us acting as co-directors, videographers and producers and attempting to uphold

Film Still 1: Ahed Tamimi in "Even Though My Land is Burning"

equality between us. It was decided that I would take over the responsibilities of an editor, with Paq functioning as a co-director in the editing phase and both of us making all relevant creative decisions together. Since I am a German-Israeli citizen, and Paq has foreign press credentials, she was also the only one of us able to enter the besieged Gaza strip and film there. Since she was not based in Germany through parts of the filming, I took over the filming of some scenes and interviews there alone.

A third documentary chosen to be discussed here is *Limbo* by Asal Akhavan (Germany 2013), an ethnographic film in which I was responsible for the cinematography and the editing. Since the film touches on a range of issues relating to reflexivity, participation, power structures, and language, and since editing and cinematography are crucial parts of the filmmaking process, this film is addressed as part of my practice-led research as well.

"Even Though My Land is Burning"

The documentary *Even Though My Land is Burning* (henceforth *ETLB*) was shot over the course of 3 years from 2013 to 2016, mainly in the Palestinian village Nabi Saleh in the West Bank. Its main protagonist is Ben Ronen, an Israeli Jew who lived in Tel-Aviv at the time of filming. Ben is a political activist who has taken an active part in supporting non-armed Palestinian resistance against the Israeli occupation for nearly a decade. The current wave of this resistance has originated at the time of the building of the wall by Israel and, by the time of filming, mostly took the shape of weekly protests on Fridays, spread across different villages in the West Bank. The film portrays Ben's involvement in those weekly demonstrations in the village. It uses a combination of observational footage from the demonstrations with talking heads interviews with Ben, the Palestinian activists Manal Tamimi and Bassem Tamimi and the Israeli photographer Oren Ziv. It illustrates the role Jewish-Israeli activists have in such actions and their Palestinian counterparts' views on the resistance in the village, alongside the political situation in the country in general.

I first visited the village of Nabi Saleh in 2012 as a protester. Not all organizers of Palestinian demonstrations invite Jewish-Israelis to participate, and it is mostly the Friday demonstrations in small villages protesting against the building of the wall or against land confiscations who do.[7] The fact that the local "Popular Struggle Committee" in Nabi Saleh was welcoming Israeli activists and journalists was my main reason for choosing the village as the film's location, as well as the fact that unlike other villages at that time, the weekly demonstrations in Nabi Saleh were still taking place regularly and had not yet been completely suppressed (as they already mostly were by the time the film was released).

I knew the main protagonist Ben Ronen through mutual friends, and he agreed to participate in the film. Ben had also studied film himself, which I saw as advantageous, since it meant he had prior knowledge of what being a protagonist in a documentary means. Ben's longstanding involvement in the protests in Nabi Saleh and his strong personal connection to many of the activists there also meant he could assist in getting better access to other protagonists, which proved valuable during the filming.

In terms of the different aspects of power relations in the film, besides the difference in treatment by the military and justice systems mentioned above, my main concerns had to do with the possibility of indirectly exploiting the Palestinian protagonists and portraying their joint struggle with Israelis in such a way as to advance political aims which they do not support. This mostly involved the issue of considerations around "normalisation", an important topic in the Palestinian struggle today. PACBI, the Palestinian Campaign for the Academic and Cultural Boycott of Israel, representing over 150 Palestinian civil society organisations, defines normalization as:

---

7   Those demonstrations are also sometimes referred to as "The Olive Revolution", a wave of non-armed mobilization against the building of the wall often named the "West Bank Barrier" by Israel and "The Apartheid Wall" by the Palestinians (cf. Darweish and Rigby 2015).

Film Still 2: Ben Ronen and Manal Tamimi in "Even Though My Land is Burning"

> The participation in any project, initiative or activity, in Palestine or internationally, that aims (implicitly or explicitly) to bring together Palestinians (and/or Arabs) and Israelis (people or institutions) without placing as its goal resistance to and exposure of the Israeli occupation and all forms of discrimination and oppression against the Palestinian people. (PACBI 2018)[8]

A documentary such as *Even Though My Land is Burning*, if it fails to emphasize Palestinian resistance, could be perceived as propagating an a political "co-existence" instead, normalizing the occupation of Palestine and advancing an opposing political goal to the one striven for by its protagonists. There are many examples for such cultural and political projects (cf. Boycott! 2014). As a filmmaker, especially one who is an Israeli himself and part of the 'project, initiative or activity', I had the power to decide on the film's narrative and therefore to avoid – or commit – such indirect exploitation of its protagonists.

"Not Just Your Picture"

The documentary *Not Just Your Picture* (henceforth *NJYP*) focuses on the political situation in Palestine as well, but from a very different perspective. The film, directed and produced in tandem by French photojournalist and filmmaker

---

8 Cf. Ahmad et al. (2015).

Film Still 3: Layla Kilani holds a photo of her father Ibrahim and herself in "Not Just Your Picture"

Anne Paq and myself and financed by the Bertha Foundation and the Qatari broadcaster Al-Jazeera, follows the siblings Ramsis and Layla Kilani, German-Palestinians living in the city of Siegen in western Germany. After the divorce of their Palestinian father and their German mother, the father, Ibrahim Al-Kilani, went back to his hometown in the Gaza strip, where he remarried, started a new family and worked as an architect, a profession he had acquired and worked in during his 20 years of residence in Germany. During the Israeli military offensive on Gaza in 2014, an Israeli airplane bombed the apartment building where the Al-Kilani family was seeking refuge, killing Ibrahim, his wife Taghrid and their five young children, aged four to twelve. Although almost the entire family were German citizens through Ibrahim's naturalisation in Germany, the German government hasn't condemned or even taken an official position regarding their deaths.[9]

---

9   Member of German parliament Inge Höger has asked the government via a minor interpellation in July 2014 to "justify its silence" regarding the deaths and was answered that the Israeli government was "asked to clarify the case" (Steinlein 2014). This was the last enquiry by parliamentarians to date and the last known response from the government.

The documentary follows Ramsis and Layla in the years following the killing of their family, as they attempt to come to terms with the deaths and search for acknowledgment of the killing as a war crime through the German court system filing a law suit against the Israeli military, which, at the end of the film's production, had not been processed by the German attorney general. His disappointment from the futility of the judicial route had pushed Ramsis into an accelerated process of politicization, and the film documents him bringing his family's story to the German public through activism and public appearances. At the same time, the tragedy brings Layla to connect with her Palestinian roots, taking part in an exchange programme in the West Bank and developing a friendship with Palestinian students her age.

The power structures which shape the conditions of NJYP's production differ from those surrounding the production of ETLB. While filming in Nabi Saleh, my passport granted me the relative safety of a different legal status to that of the Palestinian protagonists, whereas in the filming of NJYP's scenes in Europe such objective conditions were equal between me and the protagonists. We are both German citizens – although with a first or second-generation "migrant background" – and see ourselves as part of German society. Thus – similarly to ETLB – NJYP has auto-ethnographic aspects and aims, albeit in the society I immigrated to, rather than the one I immigrated from: NJYP could present an 'internal political affirmation of cultural diversity' (Hayano 1979, p. 103): showing my (and the Kilanis') perspectives as insiders/outsiders in German society, as well as having 'potential advisory capabilities in programs of change or development' (ibid.), namely with respect to bringing about change, institutional or societal, in the way the situation in Palestine is treated in Germany and the German state's responsibility towards its citizens of Palestinian background.

Nevertheless, while the risk of exploiting the protagonists plays a smaller role in NJYP, there are clear discrepancies of power and privilege between me and the Kilanis, which are relevant to the analysis of the film and the conditions of its making. An example of one such discrepancy pertains to the possibilities of travel to Palestine. All airports and border crossings into the country, excluding the Rafah crossing between Gaza and Egypt, are controlled by Israel,[10] which permits or bans entry regardless of whether the traveller is heading to the West Bank (also referred to as "The Palestinian Territories") or intends to remain within what is internationally recognized as Israel's borders. Jewish-Israeli

---

10 The Rafah border crossing is controlled by Egypt and kept closed except for special cases, mostly based on humanitarian needs (cf. Kadman 2009).

citizens such as myself are allowed entry and are only interrogated in rare cases (cf. Hass 2010). In the case of the Kilani siblings' travels to the West Bank, both were interrogated for six to eight hours by airport security before being allowed entry. Furthermore, during the production of the film we filmed Ramsis taking part in a political workshop with activists from a German solidarity group which in 2018 was reported to have been placed on a "black list" by the Israeli government, banning its members from entry altogether (Eglash 2018). While this scene did not make the final cut, publishing it might have resulted in Ramsis not being able to enter the country anymore, while probably not having the same consequences for me as a Jewish-Israeli citizen.

While Layla is not as politically active as Ramsis and was not filmed during demonstrations and political activities in Germany, her long interrogation by Israeli security at the airport proves that her actions (and those of her brother), as well as her participation in the film, are not without potential ramifications for her as well.

In many of the interviews Ramsis expressed concern that his public appearances, the film being one of them, might have negative consequences for his future career as a school teacher. While there isn't empirical research regarding the claim that Palestinians or other activists who are politically active face such risks, there are some cases that could be seen to corroborate his fears (Lorber 2017, Palumbo-Liu 2015). Be that as it may, his concern exemplifies the fact that participating in the film meant there was more at stake for him as protagonist than for me as filmmaker, and the risk of indirectly – and inadvertently – exploiting him as a protagonist was present at all times.

On the other hand, Ramsis' political work and engagement also meant there was a shared sense of common goals and understandings between him and us as filmmakers. This helped immensely in establishing trust and a sense of a common aim, as we were involved in joint political projects as well. While some colleagues voiced their concerns to me that this could reduce the needed "distance" between protagonists and filmmakers and thus harm the filming (cf. Leeman 2003), such a relationship gave the siblings essential confidence in us, allowing us to film scenes in the intimate and immediate manner we desired.

Despite the close relationship, the production process entailed power relations which must be analysed, for example the issue of control of and access to the means of the film's production. Nichols describes such power relations by asking the question 'do they [the protagonists] have alternative access to the media apart from that provided by a given filmmaker?' (Nichols 2006, sec. 4 par 1). While the Kilanis have had certain access to media – Ramsis has been interviewed by several media outlets (Feroz 2014, RT Deutsch 2014) – the mainstream media was

Film Still 4: Layla and Ramsis Kilani watching home videos of their father in "Not Just Your Picture"

not always receptive to the story (cf. Feroz 2015). With production taking place two to four years after the killing, the family's story became less and less likely to be considered "newsworthy". In that sense, while we did not provide the only access the Kilanis had to the media, and certainly not in the age of social media and blogs, we did promise them further exposure in a way that was important to them. This presents a further relevant manifestation of the power structures around the film's production, as our access to the means of production through funding, equipment, and industry connections meant the siblings were dependent on us in order to have their story told and heard.

3.2 Documentary characters: choice of protagonists as a political narrative

Although documentary film is rich with different dramaturgical forms, there are many tendencies in documentary, especially in the US and the UK, which rely on character-driven narratives that 'explore what it means to be human through the examination, and often transformation, of a character' (Rabiger and Hurbis-Cherrier 2013, p. 57). As such, the question of who is portrayed in the film and how they are portrayed is central to the film's dramaturgy and aesthetic. Jane Chapman notes that 'Although documentary focuses on real members of the public, not actors, filmmakers over the years have developed an understandable tendency to select natural, unselfconscious performers, with what is called in the profession 'a screen presence'" (2009, p. 157).

Some directors would go further than the mere choosing of protagonists and propose the creation of 'a documentary character' (Greene 2015). Robert Greene asserts that 'One of the most underrated elements of crafting a nonfiction film [...] is the creation of character [...] the shaping of a meaningful performance out of the raw, volatile and often friskily interactive relationships with the real people being captured' (par. 2). Leger Grindon points out the importance of a protagonist's charisma and notes that 'Though Bill Nichols has reservations about the impact of a star, most documentary films welcome them' (2007, p. 7). In contrast to fiction, 'a star' for Grindon does not necessarily mean a formerly known celebrity or a particularly talented person, although documentaries featuring such figures certainly exist, a recent example being Netflix's *Five Foot Two* (Chris Moukarbel, US 2017), portraying the pop-star Lady Gaga. Here, 'a star' rather means a unique and special character which draws the audience in and lingers in its memory. 'Just as in fiction films,' Grindon notes, 'the dynamic visual presence of an actor can create a magnetic attraction to the screen' (ibid., p. 8).

All documentaries working with protagonists entail a certain level of performance. Thomas Waugh notes that in earlier decades 'the notion of performance as an element of documentary filmmaking was something to be taken for granted' (2011, p. 75) and that documentary protagonists acted just like in fiction film, only that they were 'cast for their social representativity as well as for their cinematic qualities' (ibid.). Waugh sees performance as an issue of a presentational or a representational approach to documentary, and notes on the difference in the performances required from protagonists according to whether they are observed (represented) or given a clear voice (presented) and how the division of those roles is connected as well to power and hierarchy, to the question of who is performing with their own voice and who is being merely observed (p. 89).

A broad variety of elements can contribute to the uniqueness of a protagonist: prominent examples are the "quirky" Beale family of *Grey Gardens* (Albert and David Maysles, US 1975), the charismatic stop-at-nothing political advisor James Carvilles in *The War Room* (Pennebaker and Hegedus, US 1993) or the tragic-comic, self-directing Timothy Treadwell and his philosophic ruminations on the nature of human and animal in *Grizzly Man* (Herzog, US 2005). There are numerous reasons why the traits of a main character are crucial to a film's narrative as well as to its success and reception.

Furthermore, the decision to drive the narrative through main characters and their development should be seen as a dramaturgic decision, in contrast to documentaries of the expository or poetic mode (cf. Nichols 2010) such as, for example, *Gambling, Gods and LSD* (Mettler, Canada 2004) or *Nostalgia for the Light* (Guzmán, Chile 2010). Nichols also draws a distinction between the 'social issue documentary' in which 'individuals recruited to the film illustrate or provide perspective on the issue' (2010, p. 243), and 'personal portrait films' which 'place their focus on the individual rather than the social issue' (p. 244). Nichols acknowledges, though, that 'not all documentaries fall neatly into one camp or the other' (p. 246).

In the coming sub-chapters I suggest analytical approaches for understanding how the selection of certain protagonists, or the focus on some over others, influences the political and ideological narrative of a film and thus helps to either expose or veil social power structures pertaining to its subject matter. These approaches will be exemplified in the presentation of several case studies, namely Steve James' *Hoop Dreams* (US 1995), Michael Beach Nichols and Christoph K. Walker's *Welcome to Leith* (US 2015), James Marsh's *Man on Wire* (US 2008), Seth Gordon's *King of Kong* (US 2007) and Jonathon Narducci's *Love Me* (US 2014).

The political dialectic of characters and society

Different analytical approaches are useful for the study of the choice and treatment of characters in a narrative-performative work. One such approach is Lukács' writings on realistic literature and his concepts of *Typicality* and *Totality*, another is German playwright Bertolt Brecht's epic theatre and his definition of a *central figure* or *centre-figure* (Original: *Mittelpunktfigur*). I apply these approaches since both are important for a political analysis of narrative and dramaturgy in documentary film, as they stress the importance of the relation between the characters and the historical and social processes surrounding them. Brecht formulates his view on the connection between the characters in a narrative-performative work of art and social contradictions as follows:

> The drama (force of collision), the passion (degree of heat), the range of the characters – none of this can be separated from social functions, and portrayed or propagated apart from it. Those close interactions between human beings in struggle are the competitive struggles of developing capitalism, which produced individuals in a quite particular way. (2007, p. 78)

Although the focus of Brecht's work in this regard concerns fictional narrative in works of theatre, it is applicable to many dramaturgic forms of documentary film. Kerstin Stutterheim asserts that 'Documentary films correspond in their composition primarily to the dramaturgic traditions of the epic storytelling and the epic film' (2015, p. 338),[11] traditions in which she places Brecht's work as well (p. 283). It is important to note here, however, the importance of alienation effects in Brecht's work, used to create a critical distance between the performance and the audience, an aesthetic mean which also exists in documentaries.[12] Stutterheim notes that those alienation effects are meant to 'take the stamp of the confidant from the socially influenceable processes. That which seems obvious, the confidant, should be looked at with a new, reserved, virtually scientific look' (p. 286).[13]

For Brecht, the realistic depiction of characters has very little to do with the political potential and truthfulness of a performative work:

> One can arouse a sense of outrage at inhuman conditions by many methods – by direct description (emotional or objective), by narrative and parable, by jokes, by over- and under-emphasis. In the theatre, reality can be represented both in objective and in imaginative forms. The actors may not use make-up – or hardly any – and claim to be "absolutely natural" and yet the whole thing can be a swindle; and they can wear masks of a grotesque kind and present the truth. (2007, p. 83)

Regardless of whether the characters are designed to create alienation or identification in the viewer, Brecht's most relevant point with respect to the analysis of character-focused documentaries and the role of protagonists in the film's narrative is his definition of a *central figure*. Stutterheim defines the Brechtian central figure:

> According to Brecht, centre-figures are part of, and represent, a social or societal group. The figure is experiencing something that places it at the centre of a societal or social community. Due to the event that triggers the action, the character is indeed singled out from the group, but not isolated from it or their interests or fates [...] through its special

---

11 'Dokumentarfilme entsprechen in der Gestaltung vorrangig den dramaturgischen Traditionen des epischen Erzählens und des epischen Films' (Translation mine)
12 Examples would be the use of rotoscoping-filters to create a comic-book/animation effect in Ari Folman's *Waltz with Bashir* (Israel 2008) or Avi Mograbi's monologues to the camera in *Z32* (Israel 2008), the latter studied in detail in chapter 4.3.
13 'Die Effekte sollten den gesellschaftlich beeinflussbaren Vorgängen den Stempel des Vertrauten nehmen, das selbstverständlich Scheinende, das Vertraute, sollte mit einem neuen, distanzierten, quasi wissenschaftlichen Blick betrachtet werden.' (Translation mine)

characteristics and a seemingly arbitrary situation, which grows out of the concrete historic conditions, it steps into the centre of the group and carries the plot. (2015, p. 227)[14]

In this way, the central figure represents and comes from a social group, but is brought to the fore by historic events. This allows the narrative to examine a concrete character, while at the same time maintaining a dialectical connection to the society from which it comes and therefore artistically represents. This dialectic between the concrete – the person – and the abstract – the society or social group – is key to the understanding of the political role of characters in a narrative. As such representatives of their society, central figures are also not necessarily positive heroes in the classic dramatic sense, can have weaknesses and flaws (Stutterheim 2015, p. 227), or be antagonists and anti-heroes.

Lukács also places great importance on the dialectic between the character and society. This starts with his understanding of the way art deals with the real world to be an issue of epistemology:

> The artistic reflection of reality rests on the same contradictions as any other reflection of reality. What is specific to it is that it pursues another resolution of these contradictions than science [...] The goal for all great art is to provide a picture of reality in which the contradiction between appearance and reality, the particular and the general, the immediate and the conceptual, etc., is so resolved that the two converge into a spontaneous integrity in the direct impression of the work of art [...] the universal appears as a quality of the individual and the particular [...]. (1970, p. 34)

Lukács' dialectical approach to characters examines their place in relation to the *totality* of society, the sum of its historical and material processes. Lukács defines characters which represent a dialectic relationship to society and its contradictions as *typical*:

> Since the dialectical conception combines the universal, particular and individual into a dynamic unity, it is clear that this particular dialectics must also be manifested in specific art forms [...] art renders this activity perceptually meaningful as movement in a dynamic unity. One of the most important categories of this artistic synthesis is the type [...] What characterizes the type is the convergence and intersection of all the dominant

---

14 'Teil einer gesellschaftlichen oder sozialen Gruppe und repräsentieren diese. Der Figur widerfährt etwas, was sie in den Mittelpunkt einer sozialen oder gesellschaftlichen Gemeinschaft stellt. Durch das die Handlung erzwingende Ereignis wird diese Figur zwar aus der Gruppe herausgehoben, aber nicht von ihr beziehungsweise deren Interessen oder Schicksalen isoliert [...] Durch ihre besonderen Charaktereigenschaften und eine zufällig erscheinende Begebenheit, die aus den konkreten historischen Umständen erwächst, treten sie in den Mittelpunkt der Gruppe und tragen die erzählte Geschichte.' (Translation mine)

aspects of that dynamic unity through which genuine literature reflects life in a vital and contradictory unity – all the most important social, moral and spiritual contradictions of a time. (Lukács 1970, p. 77–78)

Marxist theorist Fredric Jameson further explains Lukács' concept:

> For Lukács realistic characters are distinguished from those in other types of literature by their *typicality*: they stand, in other words, for something larger and more meaningful than themselves, than their own isolated individual destinies. They are concrete individualities and yet at the same time maintain a relationship with some more general or collective human substance. (Jameson 1971, p. 191)

Lukács' typical characters, similar to Brecht's central figures, embody in themselves an abstract-concrete or an individual-social dialectic. This is a dialectical relationship, not an indexical one: being *typical* does not mean being *stereotypical*. Lukács asserts that typical characters 'are never crudely "illustrative". There is a dialectic in these characters linking the individual – and all accompanying accidentals – with the typical' (1979, p. 122).

Jameson notes that typical characters do not mean a 'one-to-one correlation between individual characters [...] and fixed, stable components of the external world [...] rather an analogy between the entire plot [...] and the total moment of history itself considered as process' (1971, p. 195). Thus, the characters are not mere symbols of their class or social group, but stand in a dialectical relationship to it and to society, and embody their inherent historical contradictions with themselves and society as a whole, as a *totality* of reality:

> True art thus aspires to maximum profundity and comprehensiveness, at grasping life in its all-embracing totality. That is, it examines in as much depth as possible the reality behind appearance and does not represent it abstractly, divorced from phenomena and in opposition to phenomena, but represents instead the dynamic dialectical process in which reality is transformed into appearance and manifested as a phenomenon and reveals the other side of the process in which the phenomenon in motion discloses its own particular reality [...] real art thus represents life in its totality, in motion, development and evolution. (Lukács 1970, p. 77)

The role of characters is thus to represent this totality dialectically, by examining the connections and contradictions between appearances and being. Reality is never fixed or stagnating, and Lukács always regards it as a historical process, a point in a continuum. Jameson notes that if characters do not stand in relation to the unique historical situation, to history itself, they resort to mere Idealism, to fixed ideas divorced from historic and material change (1971, p. 193). The way in which a work of narrative art pertains to history, to social reality as part of a historic continuity, plays an important role in its capacity for social criticism. Although Lukács and Jameson refer to literary works, the way the dialectical relationship between characters and the *totality* of their historical and social circumstances is manifested in the aesthetic through dramaturgic method can be applied to the study of documentary film as well, as exemplified in the analysis of two case studies below, *Hoop Dreams* (James,[15] US 1994) and *Welcome to Leith* (Nichols and Walker, US 2015). Both are character-focused documentaries discussing broad political and social issues in the US by following a concrete story.

"Hoop Dreams"

Hoop Dreams is an award-winning documentary. Shot over the course of five years, amassing 250 hours of footage, it is described on the website of its DVD distributor Criterion as follows:

> Two ordinary inner-city Chicago kids dare to reach for the impossible—professional basketball glory—in this epic chronicle of hope and faith. Filmed over a five-year period, *Hoop Dreams*, by Steve James, Frederick Marx, and Peter Gilbert, follows young Arthur Agee and William Gates and their families as the boys navigate the complex, competitive world of scholastic athletics while dealing with the intense pressures of their home lives and neighbourhoods. (Criterion 2018b)

Originally planned as a 30-minutes film for TV on the lived experiences of a small group of African-American basketball players (Guerrasio 2014), the filmmakers decided to turn the project into a long-term observation of the two young protagonists. With little to no budget at first, mid-production the filmmakers received a $250,000 financing from the MacArthur Foundation (ibid.), a private foundation 'building a more just, verdant, and peaceful world' and committed to 'the role of journalism in a responsible and responsive democracy' (MacArthur Foundation 2018). The foundation's grants are given out of the endowment of John MacArthur, a billionaire who passed away in 1978. The MacArthur Foundation has also funded the film *Grassroots Chicago* (US 1991), Steve James' first documentary on community organisers in the city (Stone 2014).

In order to allow for low-budget production in the initial phase of the project, the filmmakers opted to shoot on video, a technology still new at the time for documentaries and especially for theatrical feature-length ones. *Hoop Dreams*

---

15 Some sources attribute a co-director credit to Frederick Marx as well. While Steve James and Frederick Marx both produced the film, James was the director while Marx did most of the editing. Peter Gilbert, accredited as filmmaker in the synopsis, was the film's cinematographer.

was nominated for the 1995 Oscar for its editing and won the audience award at the Sundance Festival in 2014, and has received a number of other accolades. Today it is seen by many as a canonical work of documentary film (cf. Ebert 2009).

The film has faced criticism from scholars regarding the filmmakers' position as white middle-class men portraying black working-class youth, and what was conceived as the effects this position has on the film. Feminist scholar bell hooks comments that the film

> must take its place within the continuum of traditional anthropological and/or ethnographic documentary works that show us the "dark other" from the standpoint of whiteness. Inner city poor black communities seen as "jungles" by many Americans become in this film the boundary white filmmakers cross to document over a period of five years their subjects. (2009, p. 98)

Hooks criticizes the film for disregarding a broader racial and social context as well:

> Black and poor, they have no belief that they can attain wealth and power on any other playing field other than sports. Yet this spirit of defeat and hopelessness that informs their options in life and their life choices is not stressed in the film. Their longing to succeed as ballplayers is presented as though it is simply a positive American dream. (ibid., p. 99)

In this context it is important to note, however, that following the success of the film Gates and Agee were made equal partners in the film's sales revenues with shares equal to the producers' (IMDb.com). This is also relevant considering the fact that, were Gates and Agee to go on to become basketball players on a varsity level, they would not have been payed for their labour as athletes since the American National Collegiate Athletic Association (NCAA), which in 2017 reported over $1billion in revenues (Garcia 2018), prohibits any wages paid to its athletes, who must retain an amateur status.

Kimberly Chabot Davis disagrees with hooks' critique and argues that 'she seemed to miss the irony, which is crucial to interpreting the film's message to be a subtle *critique*, rather than an unqualified endorsement, of athletic competition as an American value' (1999, p. 33). She bases her argument on 'a reading of ironic juxtapositions of shots, which imply that the film's message is a liberal one about the positive value of education for inner city youth, as opposed to hooks' reading of the film as wholly complicit with the competitive ethos of bourgeois capitalism' (ibid., p. 33–34). Chabot Davis' dichotomic argument should also be called into question: there is, in fact, no inherent contradiction between liberal values propagating the importance of education and bourgeois capitalism, as long as said education does not endanger the interests of capital.

Chabot Davis exemplifies her concept of irony with the following example from the film, through a scene

> in which Arthur's white history teacher asks him, "What other techniques were used to keep black Americans from voting?" Arthur smiles and shakes his head with disinterest because he is too cool to answer a teacher's question. Not only is Arthur unaware of the history of his own race's oppression, but the deeper irony, the "unsaid," is that he doesn't realize that withholding quality education from black Americans was one of the primary means by which they were prevented from gaining civil rights. (ibid., p. 34)

A difficulty of reading ironic means in films, however, lies in the fact that usage of irony itself can be seen as manifestation of power structures as they exist through different historical, aesthetic, and discursive conventions, and the use and reading of irony is therefore subjective and context-related. Davis claims that:

> Because cinematic irony is related to point of view and to the relationships constructed between filmmaker, audience, and subject, it needs to be considered as a relation of power, a power that can affect films dealing explicitly with issues of race or with minority subjects. In order to fully understand these films' use of irony, it is important [...] to situate this rhetorical strategy in the context of the history of documentary film, with its differing genres and styles of address. (ibid., p. 28)

Davis establishes the film's use of irony as a question of form, arguing that it goes 'hand-in-hand with the structure of power (established between filmmaker, viewer, and subject) that results from this particular hybridization of *cinema vérité* and formal style' (ibid., p. 28).[16]

Certainly, the question of form is key to the understanding of the power structures in the film. However, I argue that the first step in formally analysing *Hoop Dreams*, before delving into the specificities of camera work, scene editing, and ironic means created through the *mise-en-scéne*, would be to analyse its narrative and dramaturgic structure – and determine how the main characters are positioned with respect to those features of the film.

Kerstin Stutterheim turns to Hegel for a definition of a biography as one ideal form of the epic narrative:

> In a biography the individual does remain one and the same, but the events in which he is involved may fall apart from one another altogether independently, and their point of connection with him may be purely external and accidental. But if the epic is to be a unity in itself, the event in the form of which its subject-matter is presented must also

---

16 Davis is using the definition of *cinema vérité* common in the US, often used interchangeably with the term *direct cinema*.

have unity in itself. Both the unity of the individual and the unity of the occurrence must meet and be conjoined. (Hegel in Bosanquet and Bryant 1886, sec. 2b par. 4)

Stutterheim relates this concept to film:

> Hegel and Brecht's premises of the epic have their analogies in epic film [...] A key component requires, in any case, to motivate the action of a central character by the characteristics of that person's interaction with the time-historical and social circumstances agreed upon as a set of rules. (Stutterheim 2015, p. 291-292)[17]

Hoop Dreams' dramaturgic form, covering two biographical stories over the course of several years and progressing according to this biographic plot instead of a closed dramatic form with a clear conflict or aim to drive the narrative forward, conforms with the epic form. Although Agee's and Gates' aspirations to become professional athletes do present an aim to be gained, the film's dramaturgic structure is not based around a specific event pertaining to this aim, as would be the case, for example, in a classic five-act-structure in which both might have their try-outs for a professional team as the climax of the film.[18] Rather than a build-up to such an event, it is the protagonists' daily life and the passing of time which drives the narrative.

Viewing *Hoop Dreams* as an epic film, I argue that Brecht's understanding of characters and of a central figure are applicable to the characters of Agee and Gates and that therefore their interactions with other characters should be viewed as 'close interactions between human beings in struggle [which] are the competitive struggles of developing capitalism' (Brecht 2007, p. 78). I claim that this reading is crucial in forming a political understanding of the film, since it shows that its dramaturgical form makes the film a critical reflection on the life conditions of its protagonists under capitalism, who in turn, as central figures, are not just individuals but rather stand for a wider social context.

Some scholars disagree with this reading. Murray Sperber analyses the film and its choice of protagonists not as an epic calling for social examination but rather as another genre altogether – the sports drama:

> for all of its brilliant documentary sequences, HOOP DREAMS remains a Hollywood genre film about sports, focusing on the biographies of the stars, trying to catch us up in

---

17 'Hegels und Brechts Prämissen des Epischen finden ihre Analogien im epischen Film [...] Eine zentrale Komponente erfordert in jedem Fall, dass die Handlungen eines im Mittelpunkt stehenden Charakters aus den Eigenschaften dieser Person in Interaktion zu den als Regelwerk verabredeten zeithistorischen und gesellschaftlichen Umständen motiviert wird.' (Translation mine)
18 For more on different dramaturgical structures (cf. Stutterheim 2015).

their adventures and triumphs, implying that their lives are typical stories[19], and never analysing the political context in which these individuals exist. (Sperber 1996, p. 7)

For Sperber, this formal decision is evident in the choice of Agee and Gates as protagonists as well:

> the choice of Gates and Agee was highly subjective and totally determined by the exigencies of the story line [...] The filmmakers chose Gates and Agee because their lives promised a predictable kind of sports drama — high stakes victory or defeat. (ibid., p. 4)

Hoop Dreams indeed utilizes aesthetic means taken from narrative film and sports dramas, primarily in its visual aesthetic with its high-paced scenes of trainings and important games, filmed by Peter Gilbert. Its narrative certainly builds off traditional Hollywood conventions of "rags-to-riches" stories. However, as exemplified above, this does not change the fact that its dramaturgy is that of an epic rather than a classical Hollywood drama. Furthermore, I argue that those aesthetic means borrowed from sports dramas are to be seen as a device meant to repackage a film dealing with a social issue in an easy-to-swallow form which will attract wider audiences, evident by the film's commercial and critical success, with a global gross of over $11 million. However, a reading of the film in between the sports scenes in particular and an examination of the scenes pertaining to the characters' daily lives (especially the ones featuring their families), shows a picture of the social conditions of the protagonists' lives which goes deeper than the plain sports aesthetics.

It is this picture which removes *Hoops Dreams* from the realm of mainstream narratives intended to reproduce capitalist ideology and enforce existing power structures. Lukács contends that

> For the Marxist, the road to socialism is identical with the movement of history itself. There is no phenomenon, objective or subjective, that has not its function in furthering, obstructing or deviating this development. A right understanding of such things is vital to the thinking socialist. Thus, *any* accurate account of reality is a contribution – whatever the author's subjective intentions – to the Marxist critique of capitalism. (1979, p. 101)

I argue that *Hoops Dreams'* epic form and dramaturgic treatment of its protagonists constantly places them in a dialectical relation to their social conditions and group. They are typical characters in Lukács' sense: 'A character is typical [...] when his innermost being is determined by objective forces at work

---

19 Sperber's uses "typical" here as in "common" or "ordinary", not to be confused with Lukács' *Typicality*.

in society' (p. 122–123). It is those 'objective forces at work in society' which drive *Hoop Dreams*' narrative forward. The protagonists – and their families – are positioned in life intersections, points in which they make decisions or rise to tasks emanating directly from social contradictions. Although the framing of those pivotal points can at times be read as narrative devices of a traditional sports drama – Agee's comeback after being kicked out of the St. Joseph school, Gates passing his exams for university – those events constantly confront the protagonists with the 'objective forces' influencing their lives, that is, their material social conditions.

This approach is clearly evident even in the smallest cinematic means, as the filmmakers often zoom into close-ups of the protagonists' faces when they are faced with such decisions, such as when asked to sign a contract with a new school. In watching those close-ups, one is reminded of the Marxian maxim that 'Men make their own history … but under circumstances existing already, given and transmitted from the past' (Marx and De Leon 1898, p. 5). The totality of inner-city life under capitalism and its dialectical relation to the concrete individuality of Gates, Agee and their families is evident in many scenes of *Hoop Dreams*, and the examination of its narrative structure and choice of characters is key to its political reading. Therefore, while I agree with hooks' claim that the inherent disparity of power between the film's white filmmakers and their protagonists in inner-city neighbourhoods is a factor to consider while reading the film, I argue that a reading of the film as being merely a neo-liberal fable on the American dream is partial and undialectical. The picture it provides to its audience on the challenges and contradictions of life in such social spheres is broader than that.

"Welcome to Leith"

Welcome to Leith had its US release in December 2015 and is co-director Michael Beach Nichols' second feature-length film and co-director Christopher K. Walker's directorial debut. Starting as a self-funded short, the project gained relevance and attention during its filming when the mainstream media caught wind of the story developing in Leith, which prompted the filmmakers to post a teaser online leading to their collaboration with the production companies The Cinemart and Sundial Pictures, who further funded the project (Gupta 2015, par. 5), as well as to a Kickstarter crowdfunding campaign raising over $64,000 (Beach Nichols 2018, par.1).

The partial financing of the film through crowdfunding indicates a wider interest in its subject matter and exemplifies the new possibilities of "democratically" financing a film outside of traditional commissioning organs.

However, Inge Ejbye Sorenson argues that such new possibilities do not necessarily pose an alternative to what she refers to as the 'traditional gatekeepers who still decide on what gets shown and where' (2015, p. 275) and points out the still prevailing hegemony of such traditional organs:

> This method of funding documentary content benefits and feeds into established funding and distribution models. It is the film festivals, distributors and broadcasters that gain and profit the most from such a system. Rather than providing an alternative to existing production and distribution structures, crowdfunding more often than not feeds into, supports and enforces traditional production and distribution paradigms and hierarchies. (ibid., p. 271)

Welcome to Leith's synopsis is described on its website as follows:

> WELCOME TO LEITH is a feature documentary chronicling the attempted takeover of a small town in North Dakota by notorious white supremacist Craig Cobb.
> As his behaviour becomes more threatening, tensions soar, and the residents desperately look for ways to expel their unwanted neighbour.
> With incredible access to both long time residents of Leith and white supremacists, the film examines a small community in the plains struggling for sovereignty against an extremist vision. (Welcome to Leith 2018)

The cinematography for *Welcome to Leith* was done by Beach Nichols in a two-man team with Walker using small cameras, a Canon 5D MKIII and MKII and a GoPro Hero 3. The film has won several awards, including the grand jury prize of the Independent Film Festival of Boston and the filmmaker-to-filmmaker award of the Hot Docs Festival, as well as a nomination for the grand jury prize of the Sundance Film Festival.

The film follows the events surrounding neo-Nazi Craig Cobb's attempts to buy property in the small town of Leith, North Dakota, in order to establish it as a base of white supremacists. Reports on the film, as well as on Cobb himself, define him as "white supremacist", "neo-Nazi" or "white separatist" interchangeably, and I have therefore opted for the term "neo-Nazi" since his affinity to Nazi ideology is made quite visible in the film. The events depicted take place between summer 2013 and spring 2014, and the film was released at the end of 2015.

Although white supremacism was a well-documented problem in the US at the time of filming,[20] the filming took place before two historical events which have brought white supremacism deeper into mainstream discourse: Donald Trump's announcement of his presidential campaign in June 2015 followed by his election as president in November 2016, and the killing of liberal demonstrator

---

20 Cf. i.e. The Southern Poverty Law Center at https://www.splcenter.org/

Heather Heyer by a white supremacist following a white supremacist demonstration in Charlottesville, Virginia on 11th August 2017 (cf. Beckett 2017a).[21] In order to understand the context of the film's reception it is important to note that the film was released after the announcement of Trump's candidacy but before his election. This context is also important when acknowledging that the filmmakers 'had no knowledge' of white supremacists when starting the project and 'were just really curious about their belief system' (Grierson 2016, par. 6).

The film is presented as a chronology, beginning in August 2013, with the corresponding months shown as titles throughout the film. Throughout most of the first hour of the film, the most prominently shown characters are the town's residents opposing Cobb's plans, such as Mayor Ryan Shock or Leith's only African-American resident Bobby Harper. The two neo-Nazis, Cobb and his follower Kynan Dutton, are shown mostly through low-quality amateur recordings, news footage and photos. Only at 54:15, when Cobb is in prison awaiting his trial, do we see the first direct interview with him, followed by further interviews and observational scenes throughout the remainder of the film. From this point in the film, Dutton and his wife are presented more prominently, either through cellphone-footage shot by themselves or interviews and observations shot by the filmmakers.

Welcome to Leith's narrative structure clearly positions it as an epic film. This is not only due to its chronological progression, made clear by titles naming the passing months, but due to its plot as well. Stutterheim (2015, p. 290) refers to Hegel's claim that another ideal form of epic structure is one based on a situation of war:

> In the most general terms we can cite conflict in a state of war as the situation most suited to epic. For in war it is precisely the whole nation which is set in motion and which experiences a fresh stimulus and activity in its entire circumstances. (Hegel in Bosanquet and Bryant 1886, sec. 2a par. 14)

This definition by Hegel is fitting to the film's narrative structure. Cobb's plans to take over the town are presented as an external threat bringing about a state of war, setting the town's two dozen residents in motion and activity. This feeling of an impending disaster and an external force threatening the town is amplified

---

21 White supremacist terror has since raised further in the West, with other clear examples being the massacres at the "Tree of Life" synagogue in Pittsburgh, Pennsylvania on 27th October 2018 and at the Al Noor mosque and Linwood Islamic Centre in Christchurch, New Zealand on 15th March 2019.

by the film's visual aesthetic, using slow tracking-in shots of empty landscapes usually associated with horror films.

This narrative structure, similarly to that of *Hoop Dreams*, establishes the protagonists, the town's residents, as central figures. They stand for a social group, in this case rural, mostly white, working-class Americans, and are brought to the fore by external events. The ethnicity and class of the protagonists is relevant, since there has been much debate following the 2016 US election on whether the rural white working class constituted the primary force leading to Trump's presidency (cf. Young 2017, Zeitz 2017). Through the individual, concrete personal stories of the protagonists the audience can learn about the more abstract and broader social issues, which makes the film into a 'cautionary tale' (Tsai 2015, par.4) relevant outside the borders of Leith.

After the first interview with Cobb occurring shortly after mid-film, however, an interesting reversal takes place. Although the neo-Nazis appear from the beginning of the film, with Jeff Schoep and Kynan Dutton interviewed and even Cobb himself briefly speaking to the camera, from this scene at 54:15 onward the focus shifts substantially to the neo-Nazis, with several interviews with Cobb and Dutton taking place in domestic and intimate settings. At 1:02:40, Dutton is even interviewed with his wife and young child, creating the feeling of a conventional warm family. In a scene that can be read as ironic according to Davis' analysis of *Hoop Dreams* above, the parents are seen repeatedly asking the child 'what words begin with N', suggesting that they – or the filmmakers – are expecting to hear the racist slur n****r.

This reversal turns Cobb (and Dutton) from an external, objective threat into a subjective central figure. Although this transformation was forced by the objective conditions imposed upon the filmmakers, with them only getting enough access to Cobb after he was already in jail (Grierson 2016, par. 12), I argue that this shift of focus is a key element in the film's dramaturgy, creating a process of de-fetishizing Cobb and the other neo-Nazis. It changes them from objects – a looming vague threat, non-understandable and abstract – into subjects. It personifies them and turns Cobb into a character standing typically for its social group, this group being American neo-Nazis and white supremacists, but also white American society at large. At the same time, of course, it places the neo-Nazis and their opponents as equally legitimate in the film's dramaturgy, as well as forcing the filmmakers – and the audience – into informal, almost friendly situations with advocates of abhorrent ideologies. In a late scene at 1:20:10, Cobb is seen in a medium shot sitting comfortably on his bed, explaining that Jews must and can only be stopped by 'physically take(ing) apart their molecules and atoms'.

The filmmakers are aware of this personification. Beach Nichols commented on the issue:

> We wanted Cobb to watch the film and have this sense that he was honestly depicted and that we didn't do anything to make him look like a monster. We felt like if we did that, we would achieve the objectivity we were hoping to realize [...] As far as humanizing people, I think people are complex. We definitely felt a lot of sympathy for Kynan [...] we didn't want to depict anyone as a one-dimensional monster, because I don't think that's true of anyone. (Grierson 2016)

Since Trump's presidential campaign, there has been much discussion on the question of whether media attention on far-right groups helps them by "normalizing" them and their messages (cf. Beckett 2017b, Herreria 2017). *Welcome to Leith* can be seen as doing just that. But I contend that the fetishizing of such groups turns them into something external, something inhumane, which is not part of our society and accordingly is not our responsibility to handle. Through a narrative structure and selection of characters which transforms neo-Nazis from an objective condition into central figures responsible for their actions and representing existing social groups, *Welcome to Leith* demystifies them and brings into focus society's responsibility in dealing with its racists and supremacists.

Individualism and the neo-liberal structure

Neoliberalism is broadly understood as the move to more privatized, deregulated and market-based economic approaches, taking place since the 1980s (cf. Haymes et al. 2015). Stuart Hall defines it as such:

> … neo-liberalism is grounded in the idea of the 'free, possessive individual'. It sees the state as tyrannical and oppressive. The state must never govern society, dictate to free individuals how to dispose of their property, regulate a free-market economy or interfere with the God-given right to make profits and amass personal wealth. (2011, p. 706)

In this way, neoliberalism and its focus on the "free individual" has a major effect on culture:

> In the domain of global popular culture, the iconic status of the celebrity has become paramount. The celebrity is a well-known figure best known for being well known. Celebrities 'magically' close the gap between need and desire; between those who have no access to wealth, the fantasy of transformative success and the dream of instant translation to the life-style of the global super-rich. They arouse a passionate expectation that sometime, out of the blue, a celebrity will pluck us out of an envious audience and raise us to the status of the gods. The Fickle Finger of Fate will point at us and utter the magic formula: 'You've just won a million pounds! Come On Down'. (ibid., p. 723)

As such changes become more hegemonic and affect conditions of production and financing films as well, so do they accordingly affect its aesthetic. Stutterheim asserts that:

> For some years Neoliberalism has been setting up new production and distribution conditions. This is not only changing production abilities but also changing subjects, topics, style, and the approaches of contemporary documentary productions. As a result of neo-liberal politics, some documentaries are no longer addressing the audience as citizen, an active member of civil society, but asking for sympathy and identification [...] broadcasters are first of all asking for documentaries either focussing on terrible living conditions, threats against children, women, or animals somewhere else in the world; or tell about a hero. (Stutterheim 2016, p. 3)

The dramaturgic concept of "a hero" is very different to that of a central figure. First, as mentioned and exemplified above, a central figure in an epic structure does not have to be positive, it can have flaws and weaknesses or even represent ideologies or commit acts the filmmaker or audience find abhorrent. Similar to a central figure, though, a "hero" should be seen as a device of the narrative and plot as well. Stutterheim defines the narrative centred around a hero as the 'journey-of-a-hero' (ibid., p. 3) and explains its common structure: the hero is presented 'as a human being like every one', in an ideal situation of a normal world, which then realizes he is the only one who can solve a certain problem or crisis, mostly an external threat against him, his family, or the current order of things. The hero then meets a mentor to help him with his quest and guide him into the 'special world'. After crossing over to the 'special world', the hero is confronted with enemies, meets allies, and has to endure tests and difficulties. At the heart of the 'special world,' he would meet a father figure or endure a 'Supreme Ordeal' that will win him a 'holy grail'. After this victory, the hero is rewarded and transformed, and must return to his old world, where he would start a new life a changed man (ibid.).

Such structures, consciously or not, serve a distinct ideological purpose as they propagate a sense of challenging a system and defeating it while actually leaving it intact. They are based around a rebel which does not rebel, one which returns home at the end of his mission a changed man, but to a world with unchanged structures, having achieved, in sum, a purely individual goal. Those structures are evident in many documentaries, and I will exemplify them through an analysis of two case studies: Seth Gordon's *King of Kong: A Fistful of Quarters* (US 2007) and James Marsh's *Man on Wire* (US 2008). A third case study, *Love Me* by Jonathon Narducci (US 2014), shows further ways in which neo-liberal ideologies manifest themselves in the dramaturgy, albeit not by using a "journey of the hero" structure.

"King of Kong: A Fistful of Quarters"

King of Kong premiered in January 2007 at the Slamdance Film Festival and has been shown in several further festivals followed by a global theatrical release grossing nearly $800,000. It was directed by Seth Gordon with a total of over 300 hours of footage. Starting filming as a documentary on the culture of video games in general (IMDb.com 2018), the film's website describes its synopsis as:

> A middle-school science teacher and a hot sauce mogul vie for the Guinness World Record on the arcade classic, Donkey Kong. Steve and Billy engaged in a cross-country duel to see who could set the high score and become The King of Kong. Along the way, both men learned valuable lessons about what it means to be a father, a husband, and a true champion discovering that you don't always need to win to be a winner. (New Line Cinema 2018)

The film's narrative structure as the journey-of-a-hero is immediately evident from its synopsis. Steve Wiebe is the hero, hearing about Mitchell's new record and feeling called to action to surpass it. At first, Wiebe is presented as the hero in his ideal conditions of a normal life: although he has recently been laid off and now spends many hours playing Donkey Kong in his garage, he is shown as a talented individual, a dedicated father and a hard-working American. Wiebe represents "good". Mitchell, on the other hand, is presented as the villain from the get-go. He is obnoxious, schemes and cheats, in both his careers as a video games player and as owner of a hot sauce company.

At 35:30, Wiebe embarks on his quest and travels to the 'special world' – in this case, the "Funspot" arcade hall in New Hampshire, where the "Twin Galaxies" organization resides, the league keeping video games records. Mitchell refuses to face Wiebe directly, sending instead his friend Brian Kuh, which helps to further portray Mitchell as the villain king of the "Funspot" realm. There, Wiebe rises to the challenge and passes a 'supreme ordeal', setting a new world record on Donkey Kong while dozens of Kuh's and Mitchell's supporters huddle around him. But this record is unlawfully taken away from him as the league breaks its own rules about records being set live and accepts a – allegedly doctored – VHS tape from Mitchell showing him breaking Wiebe's new world record.

At 54:10, the narrative jumps nine months forward and introduces a similar structure again – Wiebe is back in his home, apparently slowly leaving the Funspot incident behind him, when he is told that the Guinness book of records intends to publish Mitchell's score. Wiebe then travels to Florida, where Mitchell resides, to challenge him to another duel, which Mitchell refuses. Wiebe fails in trying to set a new record again, but Walter Day, record-keeper of "Twin Galaxies" and representative for the dramaturgic "father" figure in Wiebe's journey of the hero, apologizes for the events in Funspot and presents him with a special award for his efforts. At the film's last scene at 1:19:10 Wiebe is shown with his family, while his wife tells us that he is now finally happy. At 1:20:10, before the credits roll, we are informed that Wiebe has finally set a new world record in his garage in August 2006, officially beating Mitchell and becoming the world champion.

The film's narrative and depiction of its characters clearly place it in a "journey-of-a-hero" structure. I claim that this structure in itself can be seen as detached from and deliberately ignoring the material contradictions of society, suggesting that "good" will always triumph over "evil" based on its goodness alone and disregarding social and material conditions. This concept serves a neo-liberal ideology which 'transmutes political categories into psychological categories' (Sennett in Stutterheim 2016, p. 5), as well as into moral and society-specific categories such as "good" and "evil".

Once this narrative decision has been made by the filmmaker, it's probable that no actions on the part of Wiebe or Mitchell could change this dichotomy – any footage shot of Wiebe acting "evil" or Mitchell acting "good", if it existed, probably found its way to the cutting room floor. Gordon acknowledges that the depiction of the characters has 'archetypes of Darth Vader and Luke Skywalker' (The Filmlot 2012, par. 20). The characters do not stand for broader social conditions or groups but rather for an idealistic dichotomy of good and bad.

The film's structure stands to serve a distinct ideological idea. In line with Stutterheim's analysis above, it creates an identification of the audience with Wiebe while it follows him through a quest to overthrow the prevailing hegemonic power of the gaming world. But no power is being overthrown – not only does Wiebe's journey leave broader systems of power intact, such as the ones which made him unemployed, but even the system depicted as ruling the film's world, the "Twin Galaxies" organisation, remains unchallenged despite allegations of corruption.

Another element in the treatment of characters in *King of Kong* is the way the film promotes a late-capitalist formula of an "all-American" hero in Wiebe, shown to be a family man, an out-of-luck worker who used his time unemployed to hone the gaming skills which will bring him greatness. Not once are the processes which caused his unemployment addressed in the film. Wiebe is portrayed as a hard-working, non-complaining model American citizen. Mitchell, on the other hand, is sneaky, treacherous and relies on cheating in his professional as well as in his gaming career. At the end, the underdog defeats the deceiving champ, and hard honest work triumphs over shortcuts to bring the crown to its rightful owner. His deliberate depiction as the underdog did not go unnoticed by Wiebe, who commented in an interview: 'They hyped up the good guy versus bad guy, obviously, in the movie — so they made me kind of look more like a loser than I might be in real life' (Myers 2012, par. 7). This overall structure, I argue, supports an ideology which perpetuates a system which made Wiebe unemployed in the first place, as well as many who are in a similar situation, thus indirectly legitimizing his exploitation as part of the American class system.

King of Kong is an example for how not only the choice of protagonists, but just as importantly the way in which they are placed in relation to the plot, is a manifestation of ideology. This has a dialectical relation to the means of production as well, in that the material conditions of commissioning and distribution, as noted by Stutterheim above, cause a shift in the dramaturgy of films deemed worth producing, which in turns causes the production of films which promote a narrative that good will always prevail over evil and that the hard-working family man will always be the hero regardless of real social conditions, struggles or change. Or in Hall's words above, that the fickle finger of faith will simply point at him out of the blue to make him into a god.

"Man on Wire"

Man on Wire, directed by James Marsh, is a US/UK production with an estimated budget of nearly $2million which was a big financial success in documentary terms, grossing approximately $5.5million worldwide (The Numbers 2018). It was produced and funded by BBC Storyville, the UK Film Council and Discovery Films. Its synopsis on the website of distributor Magnolia Pictures states:

> On August 7th, 1974, a young Frenchman named Philippe Petit stepped out on a wire illegally rigged between the New York World Trade Center's twin towers. After dancing for nearly an hour on the wire, he was arrested, taken for psychological evaluation, and brought to jail before he was finally released. This extraordinary documentary incorporates Petit's personal footage to show how he overcame seemingly insurmountable challenges to achieve the artistic crime of the century. (Magnolia Pictures 2018)

Man on Wire uses a similar dramaturgical structure to *King of Kong*, with its antagonist being not a person but rather the legal system. In this way, instead of playing on the usurper/king theme, it uses an "outlaw" motif (cf. Stutterheim 2016, 2018) within "the journey of the hero" combined with narratives in the style of the heist genre. Here too, the protagonist *stands* for something, and this something is the ability of the individual to rise to the challenge and achieve his dreams based on sheer will and abilities in a world in which all is possible and material and social conditions play no role. Here too, the protagonist is a rebel who is not rebelling, challenging authority without undermining the structures for which it stands and returning home from his adventures in the "other world" a transformed individual. Here the neo-liberal ideology is even stronger than in *King of Kong* since the protagonist surrounds itself, loyal to the "journey of the hero" structure, with a band of supporters whose sole dramaturgical function is to help propel him to greatness. It is a parable to the stop-at-nothing self-made businessman of late capitalism, for whom other people are merely means to success – a trait perhaps best embodied in today's mainstream culture by the current US president Donald Trump (cf. Wolff 2018).

More important than that might be the film's notion of *freedom*. Freedom, in *Man on Wire*, is the individual liberty to follow one's own goals of private profit by any means necessary. The protagonist's supporters do not count in this equation, much less society as a whole. As such, it legitimizes and praises individual pursuit of happiness even at the cost of others. The protagonist Philippe Petit's then girlfriend is one example, alongside most of his other partners as well. It also propagates an idea of freedom as being disconnected from social conditions. In Both *Man on Wire* and *King of Kong* we follow heroes chasing their dreams and facing their challenges to come home changed men in an unchanged society. The casting of their protagonists as system-challenging usurpers and outlaws provides the bourgeoisie, in the words of Octavio Getino and Fernando Solanas, with 'a daily dose of shock and exciting elements of controlled violence' (1969, p. 118), after which the audience can return home sedated, feeling that freedom is within its grasp.

"Love Me"

A further example for the way a documentary can strengthen neo-liberal ideologies – and in this case racist stereotypes and patriarchal structures as well – through the framing of its protagonists is Jonathon Narducci's *Love Me* (2014). *Love Me* was screened in Hot Docs in 2014 and was later released on VOD platforms such as Netflix and iTunes. Its website presents it as follows:

> Can people find love through the modern "mail-order bride" industry? Or is the international romance business just a scam? Sincere and unflinching, *Love Me* follows Western men and Ukrainian women as they embark on an unpredictable and riveting journey in search of love. Each character's experience exposes the myths and realities of this unique industry, while also exploring the much deeper, human story that is too often overlooked.
> Forget everything you think you know about "mail-order" brides and get ready for an outrageously funny, touching and unforgettable look at the extreme lengths people travel for love. (Love Me 2017)

The film follows several protagonists, all white men from the US and Australia, throughout their 'quest for love'. This quest is aided by the company A Foreign Affair, a company which for generous sums of money allows men from English-speaking countries access to databases of eastern-European women who are willing to enter into relationships with them. The company then facilitates the e-mail exchanges between the men and the women and offers the men trips to Ukraine, where they will embark on an intensive series of "socials", events in which the small group of men is introduced to large groups of local women and encouraged to flirt with as many of them as possible in order to find the fitting candidate for a relationship.

Love Me completely elides any broader social and political power structures pertaining to its protagonists in favour of its narrative of a 'search for love'. The film features both the men and the women as characters, but its main focus in terms of screen time, interviews, locations, and language is the men. This makes *Love Me* clearly a film about Western men, not Ukrainian women, and certainly not about the socio-economical discrepancies between them. These men are followed from the outset and are the film's real protagonists. That was the aim of filmmaker Narducci from the start, who began the project by following the men on one of the trips to Ukraine:

> We had to find stories of men who had something interesting happen to them throughout the 10-day trip. Among some 40 men on the tour, it took some sifting through to find most [sic] intriguing characters for the film. (Narducci 2015, sec. 2 par.4)

This approach is visible in the narrative structure. The female characters are only introduced into the film once they become the love interest of one of the male characters featured and disappear just as quickly once it's clear that their encounter will not develop into such "love".

However, it's not only through the relative negation of the women's stories as individuals that the film ignores the social conditions and power structures surrounding its female characters, thus legitimizing their exploitation. Much more, it is through the negation of the social situation as a whole. The film claims to try and answer the question of what brings a western man to 'look for love' and partnership in another country, disregarding language and cultural barriers, but does not pose the more basic question of what makes such a 'search' possible in the first place, nor does it attempt to scratch the surface of the aspects of power in the men's decisions: the fact that their superior economic position as Westerners allows them a privileged position in relationships with the women, thereby heightening their chances of "romantic success". Instead, the film romanticizes the situation by presenting the male protagonists as insecure and lonely, attempting to gain sympathy from the audience. The men are often shown as sympathetic "nerds", tending to their video games and harmless hobbies. In one scene at 4:15, this hobby is a collection of automatic assault rifles owned by Eric, a clearly right-wing nationalist American protagonist. What might his view be of immigrants coming to the US for intents other than to marry him remains unquestioned by the filmmakers.

In this way, the film's treatment of its characters normalizes the political phenomenon of men travelling to economically less developed countries to find women, turning it into a story about love. It goes to great length to present itself as objective and equal. After Eric meets and becomes involved with Inna, the camera starts turning to her, interviewing her and her parents. It is only through Inna's encounter with Eric that we are shown some of the social contradictions of life in Ukraine, but it is merely to show Inna's and her parents' difficulties relating to her potential move to the US, presented as her having "cold feet". The possibility of Eric leaving his collections of guns and trucks behind and moving to Ukraine himself to be united with his love is never entertained.

Language plays a further important role in the dramaturgic analysis of the film, one pertaining to representation and voice but also to the veiling of the underlying economic power structure. First, it is relatively clear that the language barrier had a bearing on the filmmakers. Narducci worked on the film with a translator (Narducci 2015, sec. 2 par. 2), which suggests that like his male protagonists, he does not speak Ukrainian. This was probably one reason he chose to focus on the English-speaking protagonists. Such focus also has potential financial motivation: an interview with a Ukrainian woman would cost more than one with an American man, since a translator would have to be paid as well. In fact, the film team's knowledge of the language – through a hired translator – offered them a position of power over the American protagonists, which in turn were receiving useful support to improve their position of power over the women:

> Our team understood that in order to film these men, we needed to offer something in exchange. So we filled the gap by becoming friends, translators and advisors to them [...] Nadia Parfan, our translator and Ukrainian coordinating producer, acted as an interpreter and gave the men advice about Ukrainian culture and the female perspective. (ibid.)

Observational scenes containing dialog in Ukrainian are scarce in the film. This leads to a further focus on the Western protagonists, who are dominating the narrative to begin with. But the film does incorporate selected interviews carried out in Ukrainian with the Ukrainian women, and those are important, since they help to further the appearance of an equal situation needed to construct the narrative of "love". The use of a "foreign" language is meant to give those interviews a feeling of authenticity, and to convince the audience that it is indeed gaining a glimpse into the lives and wishes of the women. The fact that those scarce interviews are carried out by a Western camera team, which the women could have every reason to believe is affiliated with the A Foreign Affair company, is veiled as well.

Indeed, any exact connection in terms of money and agreements between the filmmakers and A Foreign Affair is never discussed in the film. Narducci describes approaching John Adams, the company's founder, almost as a sales pitch:

> I went into one of their sales meetings in these regional areas by renting a conference room. They will invite guys to come in and they do their presentations on what they do [...] I introduced myself. "Hey, my name is Jonathon." I gave them a treatment, a visual proposal to explain on what I am doing. (Patta 2015, par. 21)

The company in turn 'facilitated everything at cost for all the travel' (par. 24). A link to the film's website is featured on the company's website (A Foreign Affair 2018). This material partnership between the filmmaker and the company is important to keep in mind while analysing the film.

Love Me is an example of how narrative and structure can carry Western and masculine bias and thus mask or conceal relevant power relations. Not only does it de-politicize a political issue by concentrating on abstract and seemingly egalitarian concepts such as "love", its narrative choices bring the film dangerously close to the status of an image-film for A Foreign Affair. As such, not only does it normalize power imbalances which allow exploitation, but it offers practical service to the elements profiting from them. For Narducci, this seems to be just the natural order of things, which he is merely documenting, and the fault is to be found in Ukraine rather than the US: 'The whole notion of patriarchy is like super, super, engrained into their culture. It's so backwards there' (La Valle 2014, par. 35).

Characters and society in my practical work

In both my feature-length documentaries it was clear to me that the choice of protagonists and their narrative framing would be crucial in order to be able to effectively convey the central political messages of the films to their respective audiences. The way those processes took place differed across the two films. The story told in *Not Just Your Picture* is a specific one, dealing with a single family. But the Kilani family is only one of the 141 Gazan families who had lost three or more members in the Israeli offensive of 2014. It was due to Ibrahim Kilani and

Film Still 5: Ibrahim's brother, Salah, holding pictures of Layla and Ramsis in the family's home in Gaza

his children's German citizenship, and the fact that Ibrahim still had children in Germany from his first marriage – Ramsis and Layla – that this specific story offered a narrative potentially more interesting for European audiences.

By focusing the film on two young Germans, who were born and raised in the country, speak German as their native tongue and identify as Germans, the film is able to better expose the contradictions of hegemonic German discourses and the state's position on the matter. The film's form can be read as an epic: it progresses chronologically, following the siblings' processes of politicization and of coming to terms with the deaths. They do not set out to find a holy grail or defeat a king but rather to fight an unwinnable battle for justice for their family, find peace of mind for their mourning and to do their best to ensure that other families would not have to experience a similar fate.

For this reason, it was important to frame Ramsis and Layla in relation to their society, as Germans, as well as to their (paternal) family, as Palestinians. In this way, they embody in themselves the political contradiction which came to the fore through the death of their family – that in certain conditions, being a German citizen does not necessarily mean enjoying protection by the German state nor its support in pursuing justice. Positioning Ramsis dramaturgically in relation to the state and its apparatuses, by following his attempts to file a lawsuit against the Israeli army, emphasized those contradictions. Presenting Layla's

Film Still 6: Bassem Tamimi and Ben Ronen in Tamimi's home in "Even Though My Land is Burning"

different way of coping, with her getting in touch with her Palestinian family, visiting the country and befriending a Palestinian her own age, demonstrated that coping with loss is dealt with differently by different people. Dramaturgically establishing the siblings' different personal traits and ways of dealing with the killings works dialectically and strengthens by contrast the different paths they choose, making the narrative follow a more global and humanistic theme and thus amplifying the audience's identification with the characters while focusing on the way they are treated by their own government and society, to which the audience is likely to belong.

The process of finding and presenting the protagonists in *Even Though My Land is Burning* was different. It was my aim to make a film about Jewish-Israeli activists participating in the Palestinian struggle, motivated by an auto-ethnographic curiosity to better understand my (former) society. One of the first questions I asked myself when starting to plan the film was: would I have been one of those activists, had I stayed in the country? Or would I have turned away and feigned ignorance of the political situation?

Furthermore, my experiences of political work in Germany had taught me that one of the main ways in which solidarity with the Palestinian struggle is delegitimized in Germany and in the West in general, is through accusations of antisemitism and its conflation with anti-Zionism. By showing Jewish-Israeli activists practicing active solidarity with Palestinians, at times facing substantial physical risks, I aimed to counter those accusations and show a side of the struggle I believed was underrepresented in Germany.

After filming interviews and observational scenes with different protagonists I decided the narrative should concentrate on one main character in order to be able to go deep enough into their story for the audience to better relate to it, conveying a personal story embodying the political situation. I decided to position Ben as a central figure, focusing on his relations both to his own social group, Israeli society, as well as to his "chosen" social group, the community of Palestinian activists in the village which he sees as his political home. I edited the film not according to plot points – there wasn't one main conflict to be solved or a climax – but rather dialectically, with each scene presenting a certain argument through interviews or observation, and the following scene building a further argument on top of that. In this way, I could examine political topics, such as showing Ben's, Manal's and Bassem's views on demonstrators throwing stones at 12:45, or make critical statements of my own, such as placing a scene from a big Israeli demonstration for animal rights at 40:35, contrasting it with the small number of Israelis seen in the demonstrations against the occupation.

The plot structure in which I placed Ben is one which does not really end: the situation at the end of the film is the same as at the beginning, and nothing much has changed for anyone except for some additional bruises and arrests. This emphasized a central argument of the film – that the reality is intractable, and will remain so until there are, as the activist Mohammad says at 54:12, 'five million of Ben'.

Conclusion

Altering tendencies in distribution conditions[22] brought on by neoliberalism are changing approaches to narrative structure (Stutterheim 2016, p. 3), while technological developments are making documentary filmmaking more accessible. Such elements cause documentaries focusing on people as characters rather than on social phenomena or events to become increasingly prevalent (S- 2013, par. 5). The focus on human stories also brings with it the opportunity to induce stronger identification and involvement of the audience with the subject matter

---

22 An interesting issue, which could not be examined here due to limitations of scope, is the way Video-on-Demand platforms such as Netflix and iTunes change distribution and with it, form.

and furthers documentary film's propensity to act as a conveyor of ideology and ideas. In this chapter I discussed the way the characters in a documentary can be used either to unveil and criticize or to mask and perpetuate social and political power structures, and how their presentation and dramatic framing provide a powerful cinematic means for pursuing those aims.

Such power structures are relevant to the characters of the film and to society at large, but also to the real people who those cinematic "characters" in fact are. When a film sponsors a romanticized view of the effects of the power structures of globalized capitalism on Ukrainian women, rendering those structures invisible and harmless, this elision in turn impacts upon the lives of these women, alongside many others beyond the immediate scope of the film and its production process. A film dealing with the severe social problem of racism and white supremacy in a certain way instead of another can have very concrete and material consequences in the real world. In this way, films as conveyors of ideology can indirectly exploit – or help emancipate – their protagonists.

I therefore argue that analysing a film based only on its "internal" power relations, on the way its characters are handled in terms of dramatic structure or representation, is more of a discursive exercise divorced from real-life conditions than a political analysis. Our aim instead should be a dialectic view of the film's narrative in the context of the real-world political and social processes that it describes, while taking into account its inherent contradictions and relations of content and form. Political and social processes are in turn also not fixed – they are ever-changing and must be constantly acknowledged, researched and criticized. It is therefore crucial to strive for a clear understanding of the complex relations between the protagonists as social actors, the characters as part of the film, the film itself, the real social conditions portrayed in it and pertaining to it, and the social conditions affecting its reception.

3.3 Reflexivity and participatory film

Another key point of departure for the dialectical and political reading of documentary is the way the relations between the filmmaker and protagonist manifest themselves in the film's aesthetic. Since such manifestations and their interpretation are context-dependent, it is important to view the film not only in the context of its production but also whenever possible of its intended and actual reception. One way to discuss the relations between filmmaker and protagonist is by examining the participatory elements of the film. In turn, those elements can be communicated and made visible to the audience through the film's reflexive elements. Those two elements, when examined dialectically to one another and in the context of the film's production and reception, can provide valuable insights into the power structures of the filmmaker-protagonist-relations and into the political content of the film.

There are different approaches to the issue of reflexivity and participation in the documentary context. Probably the most well-known definition, albeit a problematic one, is found in Bill Nichols' "modes of documentary" (2001). Nichols defines participation and reflexivity as two separate modes, and asserts that

> Participatory documentary gives us a sense of what it is like for the filmmaker to be in a given situation and how that situation alters as a result. The types and degrees of alteration help define variations within the participatory mode of documentary [...] The filmmaker steps out [...] and becomes a social actor (almost) like any other. (ibid., p. 116)

Nichols in turn defines the reflexive mode:

> If the historical world provides the meeting place for the processes of negotiation between filmmaker and subject in the participatory mode, the processes of negotiation between filmmaker and viewer become the focus of attention for the reflexive mode. Rather than following the filmmaker in her engagement with other social actors, we now attend to the filmmaker's engagement with us, speaking not only about the historical world but about the problems and issues of representing it as well. (ibid., p. 125)

Nichols creates a separation between participation and reflexivity through categorizing them as different modes, ascribing issues of participation to the filmmaker's actions in the real, social world and issues of reflexivity to the communication between the filmmaker and the audience, a meta-conversation regarding not the world represented in the film but rather its representation itself. I claim, however, that such a strict separation of the two concepts is too rigid for a dialectical reading of the aesthetic and that in practice, most films contain elements and aspects both of reflexivity and of participation to varying degrees. As such, I suggest that these two elements present a content-form-dialectic, the reflexive aspects being the form which makes the participatory elements visible to the audience. Participation and reflexivity are different spectrums in a dialectical interplay rather than separate categories.

It should also be noted that besides the rigid categorization, Nichols' definition of participation as being an issue of the filmmaker participating in the reality and altering it as a result is not the only common definition. In the field of visual anthropology and ethnographic film, participation is seen as akin to collaborative filmmaking, with the filmmaker and protagonists working together. Ethnographic filmmaker David MacDougall defines participatory cinema differently to Nichols:

> Beyond observational cinema lies the possibility of a PARTICIPATORY CINEMA [...] Here the filmmaker acknowledges his entry upon the world of his subjects and yet asks them to imprint directly upon the film their own culture [...] by revealing his role, the filmmaker enhances the value of his material as evidence. By entering actively into the world of his subjects, he can provoke a greater flow of information about them. By giving them access to the film, he makes possible the corrections, additions, and illuminations that only their response to the material can elicit. Through such an exchange a film can begin to reflect the ways in which its subjects perceive the world. (1995, p. 125)

MacDougall's definition thus not only addresses the reciprocity of participatory filmmaking and the importance of the protagonists' response and 'access to the film', but also makes clear the relation between participatory filmmaking and reflexivity, with the filmmaker 'revealing his role' to 'enhance the value of his material'.

The technological advancements of the last decades have brought on new approaches to participatory filmmaking as well (Wiehl 2017, p. 39). Interactive documentaries offer filmmakers new ways to collaborate with their protagonists, as well as with their audiences, and at times, especially when working with communities, blur the lines between the two. Since those new approaches do not necessarily take the form of traditional documentaries, assessing them in depth will go beyond the scope of this research, but they are an important factor when considering the question of participation in documentary today (cf. Rose 2017).

Whether in interactive or traditional form, the question of reception is also critical. Audiences today are in many cases media-savvy enough to be able to acknowledge by themselves certain elements of how the film was made, thus making any film reflexive to a certain extent – practically any film, merely by being presented as a film, makes the audience aware of at least some of its processes of production. Jane Chapman explains:

> assumptions by the audience certainly frame the way they receive documentary. Audiences watch, knowing how such films are made, and with expectations that real events will be depicted accurately and truthfully [...] the democratization of content that has occurred as a result of the extension of video production and the internet to people usually at the receiving end of media [...] served to challenge the role of "spectator" and "location", influencing the changing relationship between creators and consumers of documentary. (2009, p. 134)

It is therefore important not to neglect the function of the audience as receiver of the film's message, especially when examining reflexivity, which by definition pertains to the film-audience-communication, since it makes the audience aware of the film being a film, an issue discussed further below.

Just as any film can be seen as containing reflexive elements simply by being presented as a film, I argue that any film involving people as protagonists can be seen as containing elements of participation, that is, interrelations between the filmmaker and what Nichols refers to above as 'social actors'. Those relations already start with the notion of "informed consent":

> A common litmus test for many of these ethical issues is the principle of "informed consent." This principle, relied on heavily in anthropology, sociology, medical experimentation, and elsewhere, states that participants in a study should be told of the possible consequences of their participation. (Nichols 2001, p. 10)

Participants in a documentary are informed – or at least, we as an audience assume they are – that they are being filmed and of the possible consequences of such filming. This is first and foremost a legal issue, securing the filmmaker's right to use the footage:

> The relationship between filmmaker and participant is formalized by "informed consent". This takes the form of a piece of paper signed by the participant as a legal release agreeing to the filming, constituting a professional "consent defence", and providing evidence that people do know what they're involved in. (Chapman 2009, p. 164)

While informed consent can protect filmmakers legally, it does not in itself ensure a politically correct or fair handling of the protagonists:

> As a way of correcting the imbalance in power relations, an ethically aware filmmaker will look for ways to protect the right of social actors. The debate about how to achieve this usually focuses on how much should be disclosed about the filmmaker's intention and aims. Should the producer always tell the whole truth in order to gain consent and maintain cooperation with filming? ... The concept of informed consent is an ethical one, for it retrospectively justifies the conduct of filmmakers who bargain over the participation that is to follow. This is a process which can include white lies, understatement and omission in terms of what is said about the nature of planned filming. (ibid.)

It is important to note that in most cases, even the filmmaker herself cannot anticipate all possible consequences for the protagonist while negotiating consent:

> Documentary filmmakers seldom know the potential problems people in their films may face [...] how can filmmakers ever have such clarity. People tend to be flattered when asked whether they mind being filmed and do not consider the potential problems of ending up in a distributor's catalogue. (Ruby 1991, p. 55)

It is therefore important to gain better insights into the relations between the filmmaker and protagonist beyond the legal or ethical issue of informed consent. Analysis of the reflexive elements can help to achieve such insight into the process of the film's production and therefore into the power structures it embodies.

In the same way, they can also be used to better formulate – or question – issues of subjectivity, authenticity and perspective:

> Our assumptions of literalness, of a link between the real historical world and the images used in documentary to portray it, can all be challenged by reflexivity. The viewer is less likely to accept the "reality" presented by the film as the only one available to be shown if the filmmaker introduces a suggestion of the process of selection or production choice. (Chapman 2009, p. 122)

Reflexivity also plays a further role in the political function of a documentary. By constantly making conscious the fact of the film being a film, not a reality, it causes an alienation effect in the viewer, creating a critical distance which allows her to politically reflect not only on the cinematic representation of society, but on society itself as well:

> From a formal perspective, reflexivity draws our attention to our assumptions and expectations about documentary form itself. From a political perspective, reflexivity points toward our assumptions and expectations about the world around us. Both perspectives rely on techniques that jar us, that achieve something akin to what Bertolt Brecht described as "alienation effects," ... making the familiar strange reminds us how documentary works as a film genre whose claims about the world we can receive too unthinkingly; as a political strategy, it reminds us how society works in accord with conventions and codes we may too readily take for granted. (Nichols 2001, p. 128)

In documentary film history, this approach is best represented by Dziga Vertov. *Man with a Movie Camera* (USSR 1929) is the earliest example of a documentary which is reflexive as a critical approach to cinema as well as to politics and society. Its reflexivity is meant to raise the audience's consciousness of the social processes of production – in which Vertov includes film production (Chapman 2009, p. 121) – in a way that will lead it to examine the world through a dialectical-materialist analysis. It is a form critical of hegemonic cinematic form, conveying a content critical of social processes:

> Vertov was the first documentary maker to argue that audience consciousness should be raised by the style of the film. Whereas fiction was entertainment fantasy, pictures of the everyday events of ordinary people could be transformed into meaningful Marxist statements by revealing the process (not the producer), in order that audiences might develop a critical attitude [...] Vertov is reflexive about process, not self, because he believed that a visual consciousness would enable people to see the world in a different, more truthful, way [...] he de-mystifies, shunning the so-called glamour of fiction films. (Chapman 2009, p. 121)

By making the processes of production conscious, reflexivity plays a significant role in the examination of the political functions of a film as well as the intentions of the filmmaker. As mentioned above, in order to fully examine those functions, the role of the audience and its reception of the film must also be considered. This role has been studied by Charlotte Govaert (2011), who conducted research into a focus group's reception of reflexive elements in different documentaries as well as in different edited versions of a single documentary with the reflexive elements varied in each edit. She concluded that

> reflexivity is met with a range of responses, which are only to a certain extent controllable from the sender's end of the communication process [...] Reflexivity therefore is not necessarily an effective and reliable instrument to raise awareness in viewers of the problematic relationship between the real and its representations in documentary film. (p. 231)

Another element to be considered when examining reflexivity and participation is the fact that those elements might also make the power structures manifested in a film appear less significant than they actually are. Chapman notes that 'These days the introduction of reflexivity in filmmaking, a more relaxed and informal approach, and the democratization of documentary have all contributed to the imbalance appearing less obvious on screen – but it is still there' (2009, p. 160). It is therefore important to maintain a critical approach while examining those elements as well, and not assume that the power imbalance between filmmaker and protagonist has disappeared merely because it is addressed in the film's form.

"I'm harboring a murderer in my film" – Reflexivity and participation as content/form dialectic in the films of Avi Mograbi

The way in which issues of participation are manifested in the aesthetic through reflexive means can be exemplified by the work of Israeli documentarist Avi Mograbi. Much of his earlier work, such as *How I learned to overcome my fear and love Ariel Sharon* (Israel 1997), *Happy birthday, Mr. Mograbi* (Israel 1999) or *August: A Moment Before the Eruption* (Israel 2002), is participatory in Nichols' sense, in a way similar to Michael Moore or Nick Broomfield[23] – the films revolve around a semi-staged character of Mograbi himself, usually pursuing a private obsession or a quest, and engaging in critical reflection on political and social issues regarding Israeli society in the process.

---

23 In *Ariel Sharon*, for example, Mograbi plays a fictionalized version of himself trying to interview the army general and politician Ariel Sharon, similar to Moore in *Roger and Me* (US 1989) or later Broomfield in *Sarah Palin – you betcha!* (UK 2011).

Mograbi's later films however signal a move towards a more collaborative approach. He himself is still seen in all of them, but he is no longer the main protagonist. Of those films I consider *Z32* (Israel 2008), *Once I Entered a Garden* (Israel 2012), and *Between Fences* (Israel 2016). These films all attempt a collaborative and participatory approach to filmmaking, and this collaboration itself is one of their main themes. In *Z32* Mograbi is creating a film together with an ex-soldier who was ordered to shoot and kill unarmed Palestinians during his military service, and sees the film as a way to make amends and clear his conscience (Shiff 2009, par. 1); *Once I Entered a Garden* is Mograbi's offer to his Palestinian Arabic teacher to make a film together about their families' roots as – in Mogabi's case, Jewish – Arabs from the Middle East; *Between Fences* documents a theatre workshop carried out over the course of several months in the refugee detention centre "Holot", during which Mograbi and theatre director Chen Alon create a play together with the detained African asylum seekers using Augusto Boal's "Theatre of the Oppressed", a method of participatory theatre (Lee 2016, par. 6). Mograbi's latest films not only attempt to collaborate with their subjects, but to make this participation itself a theme of the film, one which through critical reflection attempts to challenge the representational power structures of filmmaker/protagonist as well as the social power structures engulfing Mograbi's position as a Jewish-Israeli citizen creating films with or about Palestinians or African asylum seekers.

Since the aesthetic of those films is highly reflexive - the process of filmmaking is often made visible, Mograbi is talking and singing directly to the camera – they offer a good example of how participation, collaboration and the power relations between the filmmaker and the protagonist are manifested in the aesthetic through reflexivity.

"Once I Entered a Garden"

Once I Entered a Garden (hereafter *Garden*) was released in 2012. It was financed by the Israeli New Fund for Cinema and Television (NFCT) and the Israeli Channel 8 and was shown in several festivals such as Vision du Reel, DocLisboa and Edinburgh Festival. The film is described on the NFCT website as follows:

> In his documentary "once I entered the garden" Avi Mograbi documents a series of encounters with Ali Al-Azhari, his Arabic teacher. Mograbi shares with Al-Azhari dreams and biographic details of his Jewish-Lebanese family, and they imagine possible scenarios of return and intersections of their histories. (NFCT 2018)

The dialectic relation between participation and reflexivity is exemplified in the opening scene of *Garden*, almost five minutes in length. The scene starts with a medium shot of Ali Al-Azhari, sitting in a kitchen which might be his or Mograbi's, talking to Mograbi, who is off camera. Besides Mograbi's first sentence, the scene takes place completely in Hebrew.

> Mograbi: (in Arabic): "On the phone you told me you wanted to talk to me about something"
> Al-Azhari: (answering in Hebrew): "It comes from my view or perception of the work at this point, and of the final product. The work, the work process ... I mean, laymen like me, who don't have a grasp on the world of cinema, of filmmaking, they know that there's a script, a plot, a narrative or something non-narrative, roles, that's one thing ... but I'll tell you honestly, that's not what's bothering me. I don't feel comfortable about it but I can sleep at night. What is preying on my mind is the burden of the conflict, which I am carrying with me. My consciousness, my involvement. My despair, my expectations, my hopes. And I'm not someone who appears in films on a daily basis. So now I have an opportunity of a lifetime. Because I want to do something with this burden. Do you understand what's happening here? With this shitty awareness of articulating yourself, bringing a message across, to bless, to curse, so it bothers me, where is this Ali?"
> Mograbi: "What we did so far is try to tell the things I know. Because a lot of what we are going to do I don't know yet, and I'm very much ..."
> Al-Azhari: "Of what we are going to do, we, in the future?"
> Mograbi: "Yes. I'm counting on Ali to bring it"
> Al-Azhari: "On Ali to also navigate"
> Mograbi: "Yes"
> Al-Azhari: "Doesn't it necessitate some meeting or something? Not in order to write a script, you know, but that we sit one day for a couple of hours, drink coffee ..."
> Mograbi: "Here, today, now"
> Al-Azhari: "What is the outline?"
> Mograbi: "Now, that's what we're doing"
> Al-Azhari: "What should be the outline? What should he talk about? Inequality ... you understand, my head is very clear cut ... I'm telling you, I'm not suspicious of you. I'm beyond that phase ..."
> (Cut to a wide shot of Al-Azhari, the camera is visible on Mograbi's lap as he's in the foreground and filmed from behind)
> Al-Azhari: "... of being suspicious of you"
> Mograbi: "I'm very happy. Finally. It only took 30 years"
> Al-Azhari: "OK listen, the conflict is a terrible thing"
> Mograbi: "We only know each other 30 years"
> (Cut back to MS)
> Al-Azhari: "There is a certain unrest in my head, regarding what this thing, this creation of Avi Mograbi, will turn out to be. And not out of malice, not out of viciousness on your part, but out of the art of making, of the brain, the developments, the spontaneity, god knows what, and what if an Ali comes out which is not the Ali that Ali hoped for? What shall we do then?"
> (Cut back to WS with Mograbi and camera)

Reflexivity and participatory film 77

Mograbi: "OK no, but actually what I want to do here, is to offer to you to be my partner. I'm offering a partnership and hope that out of fairness you will trust me and that if you think something is unbearable – not just now, also in the editing phase ..."
Al-Azhari: "OK so that I will say: 'Avi, let's talk'"
Mograbi: "No, let's do more than talk, let's do more concrete things"
Al-Azhari: "We'll change, we'll move things around"
Mograbi: "Yes"
Al-Azhari: "So free. You tell me to be a partner all the way to the last touches"
Mograbi: "Yes. I'm completely serious."

As is common in Mograbi's film, this scene serves several aims on different levels. Dramaturgically it introduces the protagonist(s) and their surroundings. It also lays out a certain aesthetic form which will continue throughout the film: interviews in the form of discussions and personal conversations filmed by two cameras, showing the filmmaker as well. It also serves to present the film as an intended collaborative project and to reflect critically on the possibilities and challenges of such a project.

This reflection touches on two intertwined themes: first, on the general possibility of a collaborative film between an experienced filmmaker and an inexperienced protagonist, with Al-Azhari voicing his fears of not being knowledgeable enough about filmmaking to be able to have a correct estimation of the way he is represented in the finished film. The processes of creating a film are made conscious to the audience, as the two talk about the film not having a script and the proposed involvement of Al-Azhari in the editing phases. At the end of the scene at 4:40, Al-Azhari seems to be content with the project, pointing out that by now he already sufficiently trusts Mograbi.

It is the way the two discuss this issue of trust which points to the second theme, regarding the questioning of the possibility of an equal collaboration between a Jew and a Palestinian in the Israeli context of the occupation of Palestine. When Mograbi, in the trademark cynical way of his screen persona, notes that it only took Al-Azhari 30 years to trust him, Al-Azhari answers 'the conflict is a terrible thing'. This makes clear that the issue at hand is not only the protagonist's trust in the filmmaker but a Palestinian's trust in an Israeli as well. The political issue of nationhood, which is a core theme of the film's content, is also continuously referred to and reflected upon through the form.

The first sentence in the film is spoken in Arabic by Mograbi, who, as evident from his accent, is not native in the language. Al-Azhari answers in turn in Hebrew, a language not native to him but which he speaks much better than Mograbi does Arabic (Al-Azhari is a Palestinian citizen of Israel). In the following scene, the two sit in Mograbi's home, and Mograbi tells Al-Azhari in broken Arabic about the fiction film he wants to make together with him, which he wants to title 'The return to Beirut'. This title is symbolic, as the concept of "return" is a central theme of the film – it is a core theme of Palestinian national consciousness, referring to the struggle to achieve the future return of Palestinian refugees displaced from the country in and since 1948, and may also be read as a reference to famed Palestinian writer Ghassan Kanfani's 1969 novel "Returning to Haifa" (2000), in which a couple of Palestinian refugees return to their home in Haifa to find their lost son has been raised to be an Israeli soldier by the Jewish couple of Holocaust survivors now occupying their home.

Mograbi then explains that all characters in the film will speak Arabic, since it is their native tongue, regardless of whether they are Jews, Muslims or Christians. *Garden* deliberately blurs the borders between the film itself and the fictional film Mograbi claims he wants to shoot with Al-Azhari, and there is an ironic element to this scene: after the long first scene, in which we see the Palestinian protagonist speaking entirely in Hebrew in order to accommodate Mograbi's weakness in speaking Arabic, we hear Mograbi claiming he wants to shoot a film completely in Arabic. This ironic juxtaposition through the editing is a reflexive mean, making conscious the issue of language and its role in the power relations influencing collaboration between the two. This effect is stark when compared, for example, with the use of language in films such as *Love Me*, discussed above.

Using such reflexive means, *Garden* reminds the audience constantly of them watching a film. Such cinematic means – seeing the camera and the filmmaker, talking about the film (and its fictional counterpart) – are not only aesthetic manifestations of the power structures in which Mograbi and Al-Azhari act, but serve as an alienation effect in the Brechtian sense. As Nichols asserts above (2001, p. 128), such means remind the audience of the political conditions of society, in this case Israeli society. The question of control of and access to the means of the film's production, and the importance of that question in terms of the power relations and potential exploitation of the protagonist, is continuously addressed. This serves not only to critically reflect on and present these issues to the audience but also as a metaphor for the political situation and the social power structures in the country as well.

"Between Fences"

Another one of Mograbi's films which uses elements of participation and reflexivity to reflect on the power relations between Jews and non-Jews in Israeli society is *Between Fences* (Israel 2016). *Between Fences* (hereafter *Fences*) was screened in the Berlin Film Festival, BAFICI Festival in Buenos Aires and Cinema du

Reel, but was not picked up by any Israeli broadcaster (Hotline 2016, par. 1). On Mograbi's YouTube Channel the film is described as follows:

> "Between Fences" documents a theatre workshop for asylum seekers from Sudan and Eritrea, who are incarcerated in the "Holot" detention centre, initiated by the directors Chen Alon and Avi Mograbi. By using techniques of the "Theatre of the Oppressed" they examine together the status of asylum seekers in Israel. (YouTube n.d.)

Participation and collaboration are again central themes of *Fences*, as it follows a series of collaborative theatre workshops which the Israeli director Chen Alon provides to African asylum seekers detained in the "Holot" detention centre, located in the south of the country. As such, questions of collaborative authorship and participation are presented, but in contrast to *Garden*, they pertain to the theatre workshops rather than to the documentary itself. The process of producing the play takes centre-stage, while the examination of the process of producing the film takes on a secondary role.

Still, the issue of power structures is manifested through reflexive means in the film. First, similarly to *Garden*, Mograbi is visible as the filmmaker in many scenes. He takes part in the workshop exercises, most of them while wearing sound equipment and holding a boom microphone – another element reminiscent of Broomfield. The equipment is packed in a jute bag with the logo of the Berlin Film Festival, a reminder of Mograbi's freedom to tour the world in contrast to his protagonists' incarceration. When participating in the acting exercises, he often takes upon himself the role of Israeli authority figures such as immigration officers, improvising scenes with the asylum seekers in which they re-enact their experiences in such encounters. This creates an alienation effect: we are watching Mograbi, the Israeli filmmaker, acting as an Israeli officer hassling the refugees. This emphasizes the different power positions by exaggerating them, intended to encourage the audience to critically reflect upon on the film as well as upon the political conditions pertaining to the subject matter.

But it is not only the processes of creating a play for the theatre which are examined. The process of making the film – and filmmaking in general – is also reflected upon in *Fences*. One example is the scene directly after the title sequence – which, as in many of Mograbi's films, comes relatively late at 17:45. Following the title, we see a zoom-in shot of asylum seekers sitting on the other side of the detention centre's fences as we hear Mograbi talking to them from behind the camera (and the fences). Some important factual information is conveyed through the exchange – the conditions in which the refugees are held, the fact that they are fasting for Ramadan and that they have staged a big demonstration which was violently suppressed the week before. But the scene is not quite what one might expect from a documentary scene: the answers coming from the person inside the centre are short and laconic, and Mograbi's questions and answers which seem to be less relevant are not edited out, even as Mograbi repeats a question three times because he was not heard. The scene is over 3 minutes in length, the camera is shaky and the footage unedited except for one single jump cut. The length of the scene makes Mograbi appear almost annoying, asking too many questions while his interview partner answers reluctantly. The impression emerges that the asylum seeker is collaborating with the interviewer merely because he doesn't have anything better to do, being detained behind a fence.

This is actually the main role of the scene and its message – not only to convey the content given by the answers but also, perhaps primarily, to make the audience conscious of the fact that there cannot be full consent for collaboration in a situation consisting of such discrepancies in power and freedom, that people who are detained without the right to work or build their life will participate in anything that takes away their boredom and offers any chance of bringing their message to audiences outside the fences of the centre.[24] By using reflexive aesthetic means, the audience is not spared the footage usually deemed unfit for the final edit, and the difficult relation between interviewer and interviewee is made conscious through the editing or rather lack thereof – the question of participation and power imbalance is again brought to the fore.

Between Fences is reflexive in the sense that Mograbi continuously attempts to make the audience aware of their own position in the power structures pertaining to the asylum seekers by standing in for Israeli society and focusing on its impotence. In one of the last scenes at 1:14:35, the group is finishing a workshop and reflecting on the work, and Mograbi notes that even though it's nice that the Israeli activists who joined the workshop could play refugees to understand their positions, they would have to be incarcerated in the Holot centre for a week themselves in order to fully understand it. He points out that he will soon get into his car and drive back to Tel-Aviv, leaving the asylum seekers in the desert camp.

Shortly afterwards at 1:15:25, Mograbi tells the group that he would not come back next week since he had to 'again go abroad', and workshop director Alon makes a short pun about 'He'll be in Hul (Hebrew for abroad) while you'll be in

---

24 Compared, for example, with Behrouz Boochani and Arash Kamali Sarvestani's film *Chauka, Please Tell Us the Time* (NL/PNG 2017), filmed by asylum seeker Boochani himself using his phone while incarcerated in an Australian detention centre on Manus Island.

Holot'. This is one of the few moments in the film in which the process of documentary filmmaking is seriously reflected upon, addressing the real problematic that filmmakers are free to leave their protagonists and go about their lives while their subjects usually remain in their life situations which "make" the film. Mograbi again poses the question of the potential exploitation of protagonists for the filmmakers' prestige and profit, and of the line between filmmaker and protagonist derived from differential access to the means of production. But the scene is reflexive in the social sense as well, using humour and reflexivity to jar the audience out of the scene and remind them of their own privileged position as citizens in relation to the detainees.

As Mograbi repeatedly hints during the film, it is important to note that *Fences* has basically achieved close to nothing in improving the situation of the asylum seekers in the Holot centre or the country in general – in 2018 the government did decide to close the centre, but only as part of a wide-scale deportation plan. The film was also much better received and more widely seen in festivals abroad than by Israeli society or decision makers in the Ministry of Interior. Mograbi is well aware of this issue:

> My films are beautiful and interesting – they interest me and people abroad. They don't interest the audience in Israel that much. I continue making films because I can't stand idly by [...] to give it up, for me, is to give up on life. On being human. (Berg 2016, par. 16)

While the theatre workshops might have helped ease the boredom of the people incarcerated in the middle of the desert, the film did not bring about social change, despite Mograbi making it available for free on his YouTube channel. That this lack of potential to affect real change is acknowledged and made conscious throughout the film is a key element of what makes it cinematically and politically reflexive.

"Z32"

Mograbi's film containing the most extensive use of alienating and reflexive elements is *Z32* (Israel 2008). *Z32* is a French-Israeli co-production and was financed by the Israeli channel 8, the Rabinowitz Fund and the French film fund CNC. It was featured in several international festivals such as the Venice Film Festival and Festival d'Avignon. Its Facebook-page describes it as follows:

> "Z32" follows the testimony of a soldier who with his unit carried out an order to avenge the death of six Israeli soldiers by ambushing and killing two Palestinian policemen. During the movie the soldier never shows his face, and his identity remains hidden behind a digital mask. The soldier is shown confessing to his girlfriend about

participating in the war crime, and his quest for forgiveness. The story is followed by commentary in the form of songs. (Z32)

Z32 deals with a different kind of power relations between filmmaker and protagonist. It is an interesting example since here the filmmaker and protagonist are both Israeli Jews, and the power imbalance between them is thus very different to that in *Fences* and *Garden*. Furthermore, Mograbi is very critical of the protagonist's action, a criticism which is made conscious using Brechtian alienation effects described below.

Z32 also opens with two scenes in which the process of filmmaking and the "agreements" between the filmmaker and protagonist are laid bare. In the first shot at 0:12 we see a young woman, her face blurred, sitting on a bed, as a young man comes from behind the camera and joins her, his face digitally blurred as well. This already presents a comment on issues of participation and authorship, since the operating of the camera leads us to believe that the young man is the filmmaker, entering the diegetic reality from off-frame. But soon afterwards the young woman asks him to talk and tell his story, and a role reversal occurs. He starts talking and she criticizes him for talking too unnaturally, and he admits that he is too conscious of the camera. Again, the process of filming becomes conscious, and the alienation effect is strengthened when the couple discusses whether it's polite or not to slouch in front of the camera, thus constantly reminding the audience of the film being a film. As the woman notes at 1:42 'you already look bad in this story', the man's role as a protagonist/antagonist is defined. Mograbi is introducing his film from the outset as a self-conscious film of alienation: digital masks, acknowledgment of the camera, characters foretelling the narrative.

Then at 3:20 a further role reversal occurs, and we see Mograbi sitting in his home in front of the camera with a stocking on his head, masked similarly to his protagonists, albeit physically rather than digitally. While cutting out holes for his eyes and mouth he narrates some of the scenes that we will see later in the film. The scene seems like a pitch of sorts, a spoken synopsis of a film, and again serves as a distinct function of reflexive alienation, reminding us constantly to maintain a critical distance from what we are seeing on screen and to question its spontaneity and authenticity.

Z32 is exemplary since it continuously alternates between the protagonists actively participating in the process of filmmaking through scenes shot by them alone and Mograbi directly addressing the camera. This is done mostly by showing scenes in which Mograbi is in his living room, surrounded by musicians, singing about the film and its protagonists. While the act of singing to the camera is strongly reflexive in itself, the lyrics give insight into Mograbi's political position as a filmmaker in relation to his protagonist, acting therefore as a further critical and reflexive element. In one scene starting at 46:14 he sings:

> It's a collaboration that began all of a sudden,
> A collaboration that is, perhaps, out of place.
> My wife asks me not to film him
> Here in our living room.
> She says: this is not material for a movie!
> She doesn't understand where it all leads.
> Why help him find his way?
> It's a filthy fable,
> Not a threepenny opera!
> She says: this is not material for a movie!
> He's playing the repentant sinner
> And you're supposedly just an observer.
> He's purging himself through you,
> And you will cash-in on another profound film.
> Stop flirting with evil, you and he are not in the same boat.
> And promise you won't film him here, in our living room!

The lyrics address Mograbi's view on the case in question and the soldier's deeds, with Mograbi's unseen wife acting as his guilty conscience and a dramaturgic counterpart to the soldier's girlfriend, who is critical of her boyfriend. But the musical scenes highlight more general themes of documentary filmmaking – what is a "correct" collaboration with protagonists? What constitutes fitting 'material for a movie'? Where is the line between observing and actively helping a criminal whitewash his sins? And who is exploiting whom, when the protagonist is 'purging himself' so that the filmmaker can 'cash-in on another profound film'? The direct reference to Brecht's *Threepenny Opera* serves to make the audience conscious of the reflexive means themselves but also presents Mograbi's self-criticism: the film is 'not a threepenny opera', and Mograbi therefore no Brecht.

The lyrics thus become a dramaturgical mean which allows Mograbi a verbal way of formulating his reflections and draws the audience's attention to the filmmaking process, its contradictions and doubts, while at the same time creating a sense of alienation allowing the audience to maintain a critical distance. Mograbi formulates some of his aims in making the film:

> I wanted it to deal with the meanings of being a filmmaker, engagement, collaboration [...] I understood I must have some reflection in the film regarding my own position, my role, and the film itself. As a political director, yes, my career is blooming, I travel all over the world [...] but what did it change in the reality? Nothing. (Even and Tal, n.d., Sec. 2 Par. 2)

Mograbi is well aware of the political problematic of framing the narrative around the doubts of an Israeli filmmaker making a film about an Israeli soldier. The true victims of the soldier's actions, the murdered Palestinians and their families, remain unseen in the film. But Mograbi seems to be aware of that. In a long sequence intercut with interviews beginning at 42:35, he travels with the soldier to re-visit the scene of the crime and re-enact his actions. As they approach the village's entrance at 1:00:50, the camera lingers on an elderly Palestinian woman walking by. The soldier pays her no attention, seemingly caught up in the excitement of the re-enactment and of being in the place of the event after so many years. Mograbi stops to greet the woman good morning in Arabic, and his cameraman Phillipe Bellaiche pans to her. This moment is kept in the final editing, as it clearly shows how the soldier sees the story as playing out between him, his girlfriend and the filmmaker, ignoring the victim's side.

In the film's last sequence at 1:11:19 Mograbi is seen singing:

> *But in the end who's enjoying it?*
> *I enjoy it,*
> *That now he's struggling with it –*
> *Having enjoyed it.*

This stresses again that Mograbi himself also stands to benefit from the killing through his film, thereby possibly exploiting the film's subject matter for his own profit. Mograbi addressed this topic in an interview as well, in such a way as to demonstrate his awareness of how reflexivity can be used to make conscious the power relations between him and his protagonists:

> There's no doubt that whoever deals in his films with the suffering of others – and by the way, I don't think that's what I do in my films – also somehow "benefits" from the existence of this suffering [...] in this way he sometimes silences his and the audience's consciousness [...] the question is not whether that's what filmmakers do, but rather how aware they are of what they do and of the relations between them and their protagonists – regardless if those are sad Palestinians or happy Israelis – and how much is this awareness applied to the form in which the story is told. (ibid., sec. 2 par. 3)

Z32 ends with a scene at 1:12:20 in which the soldier and his girlfriend film themselves further discussing the case, until at some point the girlfriend, suddenly uneasy, asks to stop. The soldier replies: 'so stop', at which point she turns off the camera and the film ends. This is Mograbi's clear message: Israeli society has the choice and the responsibility to stop the occupation. But at the same time, it also has the privilege of pressing the metaphorical stop button and not being bothered by the negative aspects of its treatment of Palestinians.

Mograbi's films discussed above exemplify how reflexivity and participation can be examined as a dialectic of content and form, through which the power relations between filmmaker and protagonist are manifested in the aesthetic. By using such reflexive means, such elements of participation are made conscious, encouraging critical distance and reflection on the part of the viewer. Studying such elements can provide valuable insights for a critical reading of the way political power structures are represented in documentary film.

"I am a refugee and a filmmaker, and you ask me to choose which?" – experiences of reflexivity and participation in my practical work

Reflexivity and participation as a political approach to filmmaking concerned me while producing my own work. Since both of my feature-length documentaries deal in one way or another with the issue of Palestine and thus – through my own position as an Israeli citizen – with Israeli-Palestinian power structures, I was aware that my position as filmmaker and the way I collaborate and work with the protagonists would be a key factor to be considered while making the films, as well as to be addressed in the films themselves.

As stated in previous chapters, my position as a Jewish-Israeli filmmaker when making *Even Though My Land is Burning* had two major implications: first, I was filming mostly in a Palestinian village during protests which are usually suppressed violently by the Israeli military. These are tense situations, in which my citizenship plays a role. The consequences of being arrested by the military are less dire for me than for a Palestinian. Second, the local demonstrators can see me not only as an outsider but as a member of the occupying society as well, potentially with separate or conflicting political aims to theirs. Not only can this fact make filming more complicated, but it is a position which requires awareness and self-reflection when interacting with the local activists on issues unrelated to the film as well.

On the other hand, the main protagonist of the film was an Israeli Jew himself, coming from a similar ethnic and economic background as myself. This made my interaction with him different to my interaction with other protagonists, not only due to factors such as language but in particular because I had a much closer understanding of his social background and – being part of it as well – was well-situated to criticize it through the film.

My second film, *Not Just Your Picture*, presents a different set of power relations. The fact of it being co-directed with a French director who was in charge of most of the filming in Palestine, as well as having two main protagonists who are German-Palestinians, meant that my position as filmmaker was different as well. On the one hand, the film deals first and foremost with people who are part of German society, rather than Israeli society, and I was filming it as part of this society myself. On the other hand, the Kilanis are Palestinians and face different challenges to those faced by me, the issue of being unable to easily enter Palestine being one of them, their experiences of racism in the German society another. Furthermore, large parts of the film were filmed by Paq in Gaza, a fact which prompted further considerations of reflexivity and participation, which are discussed below.

Consequently, I analyse a third film which addresses the issue of reflexivity and participation in different, more direct ways. *Limbo*, by Asal Akhavan (Germany 2013), is an ethnographic film which I edited and shot, produced as a Master's thesis in the visual anthropology programme of the Free University in Berlin. Having many auto-ethnographic elements and perceived as a collaborative project with its protagonist from the start, it offers important examples of the aesthetic manifestations of collaboration and participation through reflexive means.

"Even Though My Land is Burning"

ETLB was not conceived as a participatory or collaborative project. During the work I became increasingly aware of the need to formulate my position as an Israeli filmmaker in the film itself and therefore sought ways of doing so. But it is important to state that Ben, as well as the other protagonists, had never seen himself as anything but a protagonist. He was willing to be filmed, give interviews as well as his feedback when asked, but made it clear that this was my film and that he would not be part of its creative process.

Acknowledging that the film was not a collaborative project, it was still important for me to reflect on my position or at least make it clear in the film. Throughout the production process I experimented with different means of achieving this aim. I filmed an interview with Ben framed as a 2-shot, with both of us visible in the frame, and conducted it as a conversation in which I was also addressing my own thoughts and experiences. In an early version of the rough cut I opened the film with a scene taking place before an interview, in which I am briefly seen setting up the sound equipment and Ben is asking me questions regarding the interview. Both these scenes were taken out of the final cut, mostly because I lacked further footage introducing me as a figure, thus running the risk that the audience would not understand that it was the filmmaker being featured in the scenes. Furthermore, these scenes had little to no dramaturgic or informational value for the film, which also risked them appearing narcissistic in form, with the filmmaker showing himself just for the sake of being in the film.

Film Still 7: An interview with Ben Ronen in "Even Though My Land is Burning"

As is common practice, my subjective input and commentary were still present in the film through the editorial choices of observational footage made throughout the editing process, in a way at least reflective if not reflexive. In this way, I edited several short scenes emphasizing the abundance of filmmakers, journalists and international activists with cameras in the demonstrations. This served to highlight the issue of foreign media's relation to the village, with me being part of this media. I found that such subtler editing choices worked better in the overall form of the film than having myself directly addressing the camera or appearing on screen. In a similar way, I integrated short moments of me speaking to the protagonists directly or them looking at the camera, introducing short jarring alienation effects to remind the audience that the film has a maker, with their own positionality.

Language constitutes a further element which I argue served as a reflexive element in the film. The interviews and conversations were not conducted with a translator, which emphasized my position as someone speaking Hebrew and English but no Arabic. This decision also had a significant downside, in that I could only interview Palestinian activists who spoke English, excluding others who might have potentially contributed more to the narrative. But it also fitted Ben's communication with the Palestinian activists, which mostly took place in English as well, due to the fact that Ben's Arabic at the time was also not fluent. In contrast, for example, to *Love Me* discussed above, I thus emphasized language

Film Still 8: Ben Ronen before a demonstration in "Even Though My Land is Burning"

and language barriers as realities of the situation being depicted, but this selection of protagonists according to language, allowing some to speak rather than others, should be seen as an element of my power over the protagonists as well and has influenced the narrative.

My position as a Jewish-Israeli filmmaker played a major role in the film's reception as well. First, based on my personal experience of political work in Germany, I assumed that a German audience would be more open to a film criticizing the occupation of Palestine and other elements of Israeli society when it was being delivered by a Jewish-Israeli. Second, my identity played a major role in a small media debate surrounding the film's premiere in Berlin in 2016 – when pro-Zionist groups objected to the screening, which was part of a political event, on the grounds that the film was 'anti-Semitic' (Flakin 2016, par. 1), a right-wing German newspaper referred to me by saying 'Antisemitism receives a kosher-stamp and the Jew his absolution' (Buckow 2016, par. 5).[25] The cinema's management also used my citizenship and identity rather than the film's content as their main argument against the film's opponents, arguing that 'an Israeli filmmaker should be allowed to inform and discuss his country's politics in a form chosen by himself' (Moviemento 2016).

---

25 'Der Antisemitismus bekommt den Koscher-Stempel und der Jude seine Absolution.' (Translation mine)

Based on the events surrounding the film's premiere it is evident that my position as an Israeli-Jewish filmmaker played a major role in the film's acceptance, as well as in the arguments of some of its opponents. This in turn helped the film's distribution by drawing media attention and leading the cinema to book another four well-attended screenings. On the other hand, those events exemplify that the focus on this position also at times overshadowed the film's main focus – in the debates surrounding the film little attention was paid to the film's content and the role of Israeli activists in Palestinian protests against the occupation. It should also be noted that the debate mostly took place before the film's premiere, meaning that none of its critics had yet seen it and apparently based their opposition solely on what they presumed the film's message to be.

In conclusion, I see *ETLB* as an example that reflexive devices must be chosen carefully, as they do not fit every form. Furthermore, it demonstrates that there are more subtle ways to address issues of participation and power structures between filmmaker and protagonist than through direct reflexive scenes. Language, communication off camera or eye-contact are all examples of ways in which the protagonist-filmmaker relationship is manifested in the aesthetic, and they can be examined as reflexive devices as well, albeit indirect and at times coincidental.

"Not Just Your Picture"

Co-directing a film brings with it questions of collaboration, participation and authorship as well, albeit not necessarily pertaining to the power relations between filmmakers and the protagonists. While filming *NJYP*, one important element of working as co-directors was Paq's ability to enter the besieged Gaza strip as a French journalist. This played a major role in the filmmaking process and our position as filmmakers. Being able to travel into the Strip meant that not only could Paq film the Kilani family members living there, but she could also act as a connecting element between the family residing in Germany and that residing in Gaza. Her visits there were important for Ramsis and Layla, the main protagonists in Germany, who could not enter the Strip. They helped them connect with their aunts and uncles in Gaza and strengthened their will to try to visit them, a topic which we in turn integrated into the film's narrative. Throughout the filming, it became clear that not only was there little chance for the siblings to enter Gaza, in part since their family in Germany was afraid for their safety, but that Ramsis' intensifying political work might also make it very difficult for him to enter other parts of Palestine as well, due to the Israeli government's policies restricting the rights of activists traveling into the country.

Film Still 9: Co-director Anne Paq in Ramallah showing Layla Kilani footage of her family in Gaza

The implications of Paq being able to enter Gaza comprised a topic we wished to thematise in the film. In one sequence, Paq is driving with the siblings' uncle Saleh to the family's plot of land next to the beach of Gaza, which Ramsis as the eldest son was supposed to inherit. Saleh is filmed filling bottles with sand, explaining to the camera that these are souvenirs for his beloved niece and nephew in Germany. In a later scene shot in Ramallah, Paq gives the sand to Layla, currently on a student exchange programme there. In yet another scene, Saleh draws the Kilani's family tree on large sheet of white paper, which Paq and I present to Layla and Ramsis as a gift in one of the film's closing scenes in Germany.[26]

Those actions were meant as a symbolic act of giving the siblings a physical souvenir from their family in Gaza, as well as simple gestures of friendship. But their inclusion as scenes was also intended as a reflection on the issue of freedom of movement and the different factors of power and privilege pertaining to it, factors which allow a French journalist to travel back and forth between Gaza and Ramallah, while the siblings cannot enter Gaza and their family there cannot get out to meet them.

---

26 As both scenes were thematically similar, only the family tree scene ended up in the film's final version.

The scene in which Paq is giving Layla the sand was shaped in a direct reflexive fashion: Paq, filming alone in Ramallah, had to mount her camera on a tripod in order to present Layla with the sand. This created a wide 2-shot in which the two sit together, discussing the gift. A conversation on the limitations of movement, the interrogations in the airport and the potential travel bans for the siblings ensued. In this way, the scene became a reflection on Paq's privileged position as a European journalist in contrast to the siblings' inability to travel to Gaza as they wish. The visually reflexive elements of the filmmaker taking her place in the frame next to the protagonist was helpful in bringing those topics closer to the audience. Unfortunately, in a similar fashion to ETLB, this scene ended up breaking the film's overall style and was not featured in its final version.

"Limbo"

Limbo is a 60-minute film defined as a 'collaborative-shared anthropological film' (Akhavan 2013, p. 5). As such, its aims, approaches and focal points are distinct from most documentaries. It is defined as a project examining 'the life situations of displaced people [...] critical [...] towards the power structures between the anthropologists and the participants of the research projects' (p. 4). This declared aim makes it a valuable case study for the aesthetic manifestations of such power structures.

Film Still 10: Protagonist Reza and director Asal Akhavan in "Limbo"

Limbo follows Reza, an Iranian asylum seeker waiting for the authorities' decision on his asylum case in Berlin. Reza is a young journalist and filmmaker who left Iran after the suppression of the opposition movement following the 2009 elections and reached Germany several years later. Not being allowed to work and not speaking the language he finds himself in a "limbo", unable to start a new life in Germany but separated from his homeland Iran.

Being a project of collaborative anthropology, *Limbo* was conceptualized as a participatory and reflexive project from the start. Reza being a filmmaker made this easier, as he was media-literate and well aware of issues of cinematic representation. The director, Asal Akhavan, designed a narrative device to emphasize those elements: a local NGO in Berlin had started a program to pair up film students with refugees and asylum seekers, who then attend filmmaking workshops and produce short films together. Akhavan had suggested to Reza to apply for it. As such, he could spend his time waiting for the authorities' decision in a more productive way, and for us as filmmakers him making a film would offer an interesting and reflexive narrative, a film-within-a-film which could make the audience conscious of the production process of our own film and the power relations represented within it.

Limbo then follows Reza's attempts in producing a short film through those workshops, an attempt which ultimately fails. This failure is partly due to the NGO's difficulties in working with Reza, since they are pairing up filmmakers and refugees, and Reza insists on being both. In one such scene at 10:20, he is sitting with a translator and two workers of the NGO who discuss if, as a refugee, he should be teamed up with a German film student or, as a filmmaker, with a refugee. At some point Reza utilizes all the English at his disposal and pleas desperately: 'I am a refugee and a filmmaker, and you ask me to choose which?' This scene is a reflexive commentary not only on conceptions of refugees in German society but also on the film itself, drawing the audience's attention to the fact that the film is not making the same distinction between a refugee and a filmmaker as is made by the NGO's workshop design: the protagonist sees himself as both, while the filmmaker is experiencing 'similar transnational migration, although [...] not an asylum seeker' (ibid., p. 14) and considers herself in relation to refugees' struggles in Germany as 'not an outsider to this community, who wants to do an anthropological research project, but rather someone who is researching her own community' (ibid.).

The way the NGO's workshops were narratively framed was important to the film since it presented a critical view of them, using them as a case study to portray more general problems with German NGOs and calling into question

Film Still 11: Reza meeting NGO workers in "Limbo"

Germany's so-called "welcoming culture".[27] One of the main points of criticism was the lack of real collaboration between the refugees, the film students and the instructors from the NGO as well as the lack of critical reflection on such issues. Dramaturgically, we formulated and augmented those criticisms by filming scenes in which Reza is taking part in activities facilitated by a grassroots organisation called *"The Caravan for the Rights of Refugees and Migrants"*, a political group self-organized by refugees. Through dialectic juxtaposition of scenes from workshops and activities of both organisations we compared the two and argued that issues such as refugees' self-organisation, subjectivity and language are treated very differently in each, although both claim to have the aim of empowering and supporting refugees.

Such issues were addressed through reflexive means as well. The issue of subjectivity, for example, was represented in scenes in which I filmed Akhavan showing Reza footage and edits and discussing the process of the film with him. These scenes were not staged – Reza's input was as valuable as our own throughout the filmmaking process. These scenes represent and make conscious

---

27 In German *Willkommenskultur*, the term refers here to the welcoming of refugees by the German state and society following the so-called European refugee crisis of 2015. The term was used at the time to promote acceptance of refugees, who were also seen as a welcomed source of labour for the German economy (cf. Akrap 2015).

Film Still 12: Reza addressing me behind the camera in "Limbo"

the participatory aspects of the production. By making the audience aware of this process, having them watch the editing process of the very film that they are seeing, such scenes also encourage the audience to contemplate the importance of people's subjectivity and control over their own representation.

Language is a further example of an important element manifested as reflexive means. Since Akhavan and Reza's native tongue is Farsi, most of the film takes place in that language. This fact – similar to *ETLB* – provided a further reflexive layer, as Reza had to switch to English when addressing me. With Reza very conscious of the way he performs for the camera, those moments made for entertaining and very human scenes, as Reza often talked to me behind the camera, sometimes deliberately exaggerating his mistakes in English for comic effect, and often ironically commenting on the events just filmed on a meta-level which appeared to be addressing not only me as the cameraman but the audience directly. Those alienating scenes were important breaks in the more observational sequences, constantly reminding the audience of the film's production and the conditions thereof.

I consider *Limbo* to be the most collaborative and reflexive film I have worked on thus far, and attribute this mostly to the fact that, being a shared anthropology project, it was conceptualized as such from the start. Reza's participation, as an author as well as protagonist, was a central aim of the film, and he is therefore also credited as co-filmmaker. I believe – and have been told so by viewers – that

Film Still 13: Director Asal Akhavan showing Reza footage in a scene from "Limbo"

the reflexive moments in *Limbo*, while causing an alienation effect, still do not detract from the audience's identification with Reza and the events in his life and in many cases enhance it. I therefore see *Limbo* as an example of a film which can be collaborative and participatory and address those elements using reflexive devices, while still telling a compelling human story and maintaining the audience's attention.

3.4 The power structures of the interview

A common challenge in documentary film is the attempt to convey to the audience important information which cannot be obtained through the mere visual documentation of events. This can either be information pertaining to events taking place before the filming process began, to the emotions and opinions of the protagonists, or to abstract facts which are difficult to demonstrate as part of an audio-visual diegesis of concrete events playing out in front of the camera. This is where active extraction of information from the protagonists becomes valuable for the filmmakers. The most common form for such extraction of information is the interview.

Although any method of provoking answers from a protagonist might fall under the category of an interview, the term "interview" has established itself as describing a more formal and direct method of questioning. It is therefore important to define what an interview actually is, what parallels it has in other disciplines, and what implications it has in the context of political power structures, especially between the filmmaker/interviewer and the protagonist/interviewee.

Historical emergence of the interview form

Leger Grindon claims that 'The interview begins to assume prominence only during the television era and after effective mobile sound equipment becomes employed around 1960' (2007, p. 4), and places it in a historical dialectic by arguing that 'Two streams of influence have shaped the contemporary documentary interview: the French cinema verité tradition, with roots in ethnography, and the American political heritage, with ties to television journalism' (ibid.). While this is certainly true regarding the prominence of the form, Grindon does not mention films such as *Housing Problems* (Elton and Anstey, UK 1935) which is a prominent example of the first use of the documentary interview in the West and had a canonical influence on film and television (McLane 2012, p. 84), or Soviet films such as *Three Songs for Lenin* (Vertov, USSR 1934) and *Komsomol Patron of Electrification* (Shub, USSR 1932), both apparently unknown to Elton or Anstey at the time of filming *Housing Problems* (Winston 2008, p. 51).

As mentioned in Chapter 3, *Housing Problems* owes in many ways its groundbreaking form as harbinger of on-location interviews to its sponsor, the British Commercial Gas Association. The film was made possible by this commissioning in order to expose the troublesome living conditions of people without proper gas heating and the necessity of urban renewal. Brian Winston says of the film 'The victim documentary par excellence [...] brings together the techniques that had been discovered for the use of synchronous sound and the "problem moment" structure' (2008, p. 49–50), thus pointing to the dialectical connection between the interview as form and the political context of the film's dramaturgy. Winston defines the concept of the 'problem moment' structure:

> The slums are but a moment – what might be termed a "problem moment" – in the unfolding history of the nation, a moment that will pass [...] This "Problem moment" structure allows for a social ill to be covered (permitting a radical reading of the final film) while at the same time denying that the ill has real causes and effects (permitting conservative funding for the film). (p. 48)

The interview is a prime example of an aesthetic device useful for such a structure. People speak to the camera on the social ills plaguing them, seemingly of their own accord, but the decision whether to examine the real causes of those ills remains entirely with the filmmaker. The (documentary) interview has long been a tool of social research (cf. Mayhew 1861) and much debate exists on its relation to society and its potential for social change, which exceeds the scope of this paper. An example of such debate would be the public discussion between Klaus Kreimeier and Klaus Wildenhahn (cf. Hohenberger 1992).

Aesthetic and form of the interview

An interview can take many aesthetic forms, all of which have a dialectical relation with the respective content. While basically any attempt to glean and record information from the protagonist can be seen as an interview, it is useful to examine and define the different common forms an interview can take.

Talking Head

Perhaps the most common form of a visual interview, prominent in television but common in film as well, is the so-called "talking head" form. In this form, the interviewee is neatly framed, usually in front of a neutral background and in a medium shot or a close-up, answering questions while addressing the filmmaker sitting close to the camera. In this way, the eye-line of the interviewee is in close proximity to the camera, creating the feeling that she is "almost" talking to the audience, but still past them. This is a well-known convention in fiction film: in order to create intimacy with a character, but still deny the presence of the camera in order to maintain the illusion of reality, a close-up of a dialogue scene would often be set up in a similar way. This form of interview is well established in nonfiction, with a clear exception being the television expert interview, in which the interviewee is asked to look directly into the camera while usually hearing the questions through an ear piece, in order to maintain a similar frame as the interviewer.

One filmmaker who has repeatedly broken the documentary eye-line convention, borrowing from the TV aesthetic of looking directly in the camera for his documentary work, is Errol Morris with his "Interrotron", a device projecting a live feed of the interviewer's face into a teleprompter positioned in front of the camera, so that the interviewee, when addressing the projected image of the interviewer, actually stares into the lens and therefore looks "directly" at the audience (Resha 2015, p. 171).[28] This form breaks the voyeuristic and distanced effect of the common "talking head" form, creating an alienation effect through the interviewee's seemingly direct address of the audience.

---

28 A more recent example of such an approach can be seen in Chris Smith's *Jim & Andy: The Great Beyond* (US 2017), in which actor Jim Carrey is interviewed while looking directly at the camera, intercut with a second camera from the side.

This common method of a "talking head" interview, regardless of eye-line, results in very clear, albeit at times overlooked, power relations between the interviewer and the interviewee. In terms of form, those power relations are manifested predominantly through the question of *who* is to be seen.[29] In terms of content, through the question of *what* is to be seen: which answers are selected to be presented. In this constellation, the filmmaker is hidden behind (or rather slightly to the side of) the camera, protected by her invisibility. Not only is the actual visual figure of the filmmaker absent from the diegesis, but it is also very common to edit out her questions and create the illusion of an interviewee speaking solely on her own accord, a method which allows for further manipulation of content.

Bill Nichols discusses the "talking head" form:

> A specific agenda comes into play and the information extracted from the exchange may be placed within a larger frame of reference to which it contributes a distinct piece of factual information or affective overtone [...] the common interview normally requires subjects to provide a frontal view of themselves and generally discipline their bodies to oblige the camera's requirements regarding depth of field and angle of view. The individual identity, autobiographical background, or idiosyncratic qualities of those interviewed become secondary to an external referent: some aspect of the historical world to which they can contribute special knowledge. (1991, p. 52–53)

Of course, the use of the "talking head" form in itself cannot be examined politically divorced from other means, and filmmakers can have 'a specific agenda' and manipulatively place the footage in 'a larger frame of reference' using other forms of interview as well. Nichols claims that 'No one-to-one correlation exists between form and content with regard to the interview any more than to low-angle shots or high-key lighting. But each choice of spatio-temporal configuration between filmmaker and interviewee carries implications and a potential political charge' (ibid., p. 51).

Vox Pop

Another classic form of the interview, and one which places even more focus on the act of interviewing itself, is the so-called "Vox Populi" or "vox pop", literally the voice of the people. This is usually done by conducting what is also called a "man on the street" interview, in which the filmmaker addresses people uninvolved with the film in a public space:

---

[29] The question of seeing and being seen as a manifestation of power structures is discussed in further detail in section 4.5.

In Film and television, consultation with the ordinary person in the street is referred to as 'vox pop'. This phrase comes from the Latin 'Vox Populi': the voice of the people. Typically, the scene behind the person being interviewed will establish his or her status as the man or woman in the street. (Nicholas and Price 1998, p. 126)

The filmmaker would address a passer-by, asking them directly if they would mind being interviewed and posing the questions with camera and microphone clearly directed at the person. The control of the filmmaker over the discourse, especially in television, is then similar to a "talking head" situation, with the questions and the image of the director often left out in the editing. In many cases an outstretched hand holding a microphone in the frame will be the only presence of the filmmaker seen in the edited interview, although sometimes the interview might also be framed as a 2-shot with the filmmaker/journalist clearly visible.

Vox pop, as its name suggests, aesthetically conveys a sense of spontaneity and an impression of the real and authentic and has a 'certain representative legitimacy' and a 'populist touch' (Hackett 1985, p. 259). I assert that this appearance of authenticity can also serve to further veil the processes of editing and narrative manipulations: since vox pop creates a clear visual and contextual connection between the interviewee and the location, it also often serves to suggest certain ideas regarding an area, a neighbourhood or a population.

How vox pop can be used to suggest such ideas regarding a population can be exemplified through a media format often utilizing this form, the video or news report. In 2016, a crew from the German magazine "Die Welt" created the online video *Das Experiment* (Germany 2016). In it, what appears to be a religious Jew, wearing a black orthodox Kippa, is filmed in a refugee accommodation in Berlin. The person engages various refugees in short vox pop interviews in front of the camera, asking them questions about Israel and Palestine. An interview at the end of the segment, edited as a monologue, as well as superimposed titles throughout the video suggest a rising danger of antisemitism on the part of the newly arrived Syrian refugees and frame the refugee accommodation as a hotbed of anti-Jewish racism.

Without further knowledge, this seems to be the case. No information is given explaining that the person conducting the interviews – besides not being religious – is in fact employed by a political lobby group which has the aim of propagating a certain political definition of antisemitism in Germany (Ofir 2016, par.1). The audience has no way of knowing to what extent the interviews are edited or even how many of the interviewees have enough command of English or German language to fully understand what they've been asked. This is one example of how vox pop as a form is used to suggest authenticity and unmediated depiction of current events and tendencies in a particular place or society.

Another interesting aspect of vox pop is its propensity for incorporating a wide range of reflexive means, which can enable filmmakers to present their position or political affiliation and therefore, without negating or deconstructing it, makes their position or partisanship visible and present in the edited film. One example of such use of vox pop is Patricio Guzmán's three-part documentary *Battle of Chile* (Chile 1975, 1976, 1979). The film consists of many scenes in which Guzmán and his small team tour the country, documenting the events leading to the military coup of 1973. They engage in short interviews with people from different sides of the ever-growing political chasm in the country, from workers and trade unionists to bourgeois capitalists and pro-fascists. Many of Guzmán's questions are left audible in the edited film, with him often also visible. Guzmán's appearances in the vox pop sequences become a reflexive device:

> When Guzmán is conducting vox pops, he is leading the camera among the crowd; we often hear his instructions to the camera to turn on or to follow him, and it gives a tremendous sense of being there (or in Spanish, *presenciar*, to be a witnessing presence). (Chanan 2007, p. 205)

Camera movement is used in conjunction with the interviews to comment and contextualize the information extracted from the protagonists: in one scene at 12:50 of part 1, the crew enters the home of a middle-class supporter of the conservative Christian Democrat party under the pretence of being a TV team who would like to film from her balcony. While Guzmán engages the lady in interview, and she explains her support to the conservatives, his cinematographer, Jorge Müller Silva (who later disappeared in Pinochet's torture cells), pans away from her in a fashion uncommon in a traditional vox pop form, but one which is consistently applied throughout the film. The camera presents the room, juxtaposing the interviewee's answers with her luxurious flat. In this way, Müller Silva's camera positions the interviewee's comments in relation to her class and to the overall dialectic of class tensions in Chile. Referring to another scene in the film, Chanan notes that 'the camera's presence is witness to the truth of the moment – a moment in which the individual belongs most fully to the collective' (p. 206–207). This observation holds true for this scene as well.

The vox pop sequence in *Battle of Chile* should be examined in the context of the overall structure of the film as well, in which Guzmán's political position is quite clear, thus giving the audience further knowledge and context to better judge the vox pop interviews themselves.

Conversation, dialogue or pseudo-dialogue

An interview can also take a seemingly more balanced form, one similar to a real-life conversation. Nichols refers to such a form as a 'dialogue' or, more accurately, a 'pseudo-dialogue':

> A more structured interaction between filmmaker and social actor where both are present and visible may give the impression of "dialogue", again in quotes because of the hierarchy of control that guides and direct the exchange [...] This form of exchange might also be termed "pseudo-dialogue" since the interview format prohibits full reciprocity or equality between the participants [...] The resulting impression of a pseudo-dialogue disguises the degree to which such exchanges are, in fact, as highly formalized here as they are in other institutional contexts. (1991, p. 52)

An example for such a "pseudo-dialogue" can be found in Julia Query's and Vicki Funari's *Live Nude Girls, Unite!* (US 2000). Query documents her and her co-worker's attempts at unionizing their workplace at a San Francisco strip club. At one point in the film, she finds herself speaking about their labour dispute in a conference on sex work, in which her mother, a prominent psychologist working with sex workers, speaks as well. The situation forces her to tell her mother for the first time that she is working as a stripper. This conversation at 50:00, taking place in a hotel room, escalates to a fight between mother and daughter. The scene has the appearance of a dialogue, and the fact that Query is framed together with her mother creates a sense of equality. At the same time, it is Query who initiated the talk and she who decides on how this conversation will be used and framed in the final film – framed in the literal sense as well, when at some point in the argument Query calls Funari, operating the camera, to come closer and get a better shot.

The Masked Interview

A further interesting form, albeit not a very common one, is what Nichols terms the 'masked interview', a definition sometimes falsely interpreted as pertaining to any interview in which the presence of the filmmaker is cut or framed out as in a "talking head" situation (Summerhayes 2004, p. 21). Nichols defines it as follows:

> A variation on "mere" conversation, even less obviously organized by the filmmaker, is the "masked interview". In this case the filmmaker is both off screen and unheard. Equally significant, the interviewee no longer addresses the filmmaker off screen but engages in conversation with another social actor [...] the impression rendered is very hard to differentiate from ordinary conversations of the sort found in observational films. The key difference, however, is that we observe an implanted conversation. (1991, p. 51-52)

The "masked interview" is an example of a way in which not only can the filmmakers affect the discursive interaction and the protagonist's speech, but they are also able to hide this interaction in the finished film and present the situation as observational and even spontaneous. In the part discussing my practical work below I will exemplify this form using a scene from *Even Though My Land is Burning*.

Theoretical approaches to different interview forms

Nichols places the different forms of an interview situation on a spectrum. At one end, he sees the '"conversation", a free exchange between filmmaker and subject that seems to follow no predetermined course and to address no clearly specified agenda' (1991, p. 51). He notes, though, that the mere act of filming transforms such a conversation into something else. The 'masked interview' follows as a variation on the conversation, albeit one in which the filmmaker is not present. Then comes the 'dialogue' or the 'pseudo-dialogue'. Last on the spectrum comes the common interview, which correlates in most cases to the "talking head" form (ibid., p. 51–53).

Nichols' spectrum offers a way of categorizing interview forms. I assert, however, that such a categorization is not enough to address the full role of the interview situation in the overall dramaturgic structure and dialectic of a film, its narrative and the way authorial power is exercised on the interviewee's speech. A method which considers wide and multiple, overlapping contexts is needed.

Leger Grindon (2007) offers different categories which I argue are more useful for this aim, since they also take into consideration the wider context of the interview in the finished film itself. He categorizes interviews according to *presence, perspective, pictorial context, performance* and *polyvalence* (ibid., p. 6).

Presence pertains to how present the director is in terms of framing, editing and sound. I would add that this category should not only be understood in terms of physical presence in the edited film but can also be extended to implicit presence, in terms of eye-line, formulation of answers, body language etc.

Perspective is a category of form and 'concerns setting and camera position' (ibid., p. 7). *Pictorial context* refers to 'the independent imagery that complements or works in counterpoint to the verbal testimony of the speaker' (ibid.). It is a category pertaining to editing: a question of which shots or scenes complement or contradict the speech. This is an important category, since it touches on the topic of the dialectics of editorial context, albeit more in regard to the sequence and scene than to the overall dramaturgic structure. Most films by Errol Morris present good examples of use of pictorial context, since Morris tends to counterpoint or strengthen his protagonists' statements with highly stylized shots, which might appear to be metaphorical or commentating in relation to the speech. Grindon mentions Moriss' *The Thin Blue Line* (US 1988) as an example (ibid.). Another example for pictorial context, though not through editing, is the camera work during vox pop interviews in *Battle of Chile*, discussed above, and the way it comments and contextualizes the speech "in-the-shot", using pans and close-ups of the interviewee's surroundings to provide political context.

Performance is a category which is often insufficiently addressed in the analysis of documentary film. Grindon notes that 'In addition to speech, facial expression, hand gestures, body language, and clothing characterize the interviewee.' (ibid.). This is an important category since we must bear in mind that protagonists are usually not only chosen for their lived experiences or for their place in society, but also for their star-quality (ibid.). Many documentaries are built around their protagonists, and their selection is no less important than in fiction film (cf. Catliff and Granville 2013).

An example of the effect of different levels of performance – although a TV documentary rather than a theatrical film – is Marc Levin's *Class Divide* (US 2015). The film documents two groups of New York teenagers, one living in a social housing project and one attending the rich, elite school across the street. Levin criss-crosses through different interviews with the teenagers. While most of his protagonists from the private school appear pale and timid, well-articulated but mostly lacking confidence, the "performance" of seven-year-old Rosa from the housing block is colourful and lively, overshadowing their characters with her adult-like observations, "cheeky" speaking style and energetic body language. This difference in performance influences the portrayal of the teenagers – the private school students are full of doubt, seemingly weighed down by a "white man's burden" of being born on the privileged side of the class divide and groomed for leadership and success, while the social housing children are presented as having a love of life and a maturity only attainable through the hardships of working-class existence.

I argue that through this imbalance Levin is actually veiling the class imbalance shown in his film. The way those different performances are framed serves to romanticize poverty in a way reminiscent of what Winston defines as 'victim documentaries' (2008, p. 46–54).

Grindon's last category, *polyvalence*, is useful in examining interview sequences in the context of their dialectic relation to the narrative and dramaturgic structure:

> Polyvalence is distinct from the other four because rather than being an aspect of the interview's design it emerges as a result of the whole. Polyvalence gauges the interview's overall formal effect. Here the choice arises between affirming or undermining the authority of the interviewee... A difference may also arise between the filmmaker and subject, especially if the interviewee is given a genuine opportunity to contest the filmmaker. (2007, p. 8)

Since Grindon's categories offer a method of analysing interviews in a dramaturgic context rather than a purely visually formal one, taking the film as a whole into consideration, I assert they provide an important tool when examining the power structures manifested in interview scenes and interview-based documentaries.

"The Fog of War"

While interviews are often used to give different perspectives on the film's subject, they can also be used as a more central aesthetic device to drive the narrative. Errol Morris' *The Fog of War: Eleven Lessons from the Life of Robert S. McNamara* (US 2004), briefly discussed above, is an interesting example as it uses its protagonist Robert McNamara's voice as a narrating device throughout the film, in a way similar to the "voice-of-god" which 'addresses the viewer directly, with titles or voices that advance an argument about the historical world' (Nichols 1991, p. 34).

The Fog of War earned Morris an Oscar for best documentary in 2004 and grossed over 4 Million dollars in the US. The film intercuts interview footage with McNamara, a former US Secretary of State for Defence, filmed using Morris' "Interrotron" explained above, with visual sequences of archival footage and observational and studio construction footage shot specifically for the film.

As David Resha notes (2015, p. 169), this is Morris' first film in which he exclusively uses the speech of a single interviewee, having used this technique previously in his TV-series *First Person* (US 2000). While Morris appears to be providing McNamara with the opportunity to narrate his own life story, he places carefully selected statements from several days of interviews (ibid., p. 170) together with his metaphorically laden visuals and Phillip Glass's dramatic music.

Morris' intercutting of the interviews with visuals exemplifies the importance of Grindon's category of pictorial context in discussing the film. In some sequences, such as at 35:15, images of documents signed by McNamara or archival audio recording are edited together with his statements regarding his lack of responsibility for and knowledge of specific military actions. The pictorial context contradicts McNamara's statements, showing he indeed knew of these events, and serves to provide Morris' own commentary on the interviews.

Another example are the studio shots showing huge domino tiles on a map of the world at 41:30, alluding to the US's cold war "Truman Doctrine" of the "Domino Effect" in relation to the spread of communism in Asia. These shots invert the interpretation of the doctrine and present the Domino Effect as a visualization of US interventionism in the area (Miller 2011, p. 35).

The importance of polyvalence is also exemplified here. Morris repeatedly uses McNamara's statements regarding the issue of mistakes and accountability and lets McNamara stress again and again that military commanders always make mistakes. This repetition makes the issue of accountability a central theme of the film, drawing the audience's attention to the question of McNamara's responsibility during the Vietnam war. In this way, even though he insists on minimizing his responsibility for the breakout of war or the atrocities committed by the US military throughout it, Morris' editorial voice repeatedly contradicts his assertions.

The Fog of War is an interesting example of how a filmmaker can retain power over the protagonist when utilizing an aesthetic form which at first might seem to give the protagonist power to shape the narrative. Having McNamara's own voice lead the film thus veils the fact that it is indeed Morris' voice, not McNamara's, which through the editorial process has the power over McNamara's ultimate representation. This, however, does not pose a problem for Morris:

> McNamara is telling you a very, very, *very* powerful story, a very important story. But I like to think that it's been communicated visually. The voice-over, the visuals combine in a way that a story is told [...] in telling history, you have to chart a course through a morass of material. You have to tell a story, and you have to communicate the story powerfully. (in Cunningham 2014, p. 60)

The power relations of interviews

Nichols establishes that protagonists in an interview situation

> give their testimony within a frame they cannot control and may not understand. The tone and perspective are not theirs to determine. Their task is to contribute evidence to someone else's argument, and when well done [...] our attention is not on how the filmmaker *uses* witnesses to make a point but on the effectiveness of the argument itself. (1991, p. 37)

The testimony thus becomes content like any other, and the way in which it can be framed, used, presented and manipulated remains to a large extent in the hands of the filmmaker. Furthermore, Nichols points out how the character of the interview form draws the audience's attention to the filmmaker's own arguments and away from the ways in which the speech is manipulated, contextualized or framed. It is important to note that it is not only the "tone and perspective" which the interviewees cannot determine, but also the setting and agenda of the interview as a whole, such as which questions are asked and which topics are addressed, elements crucial to the overall impact of the interview. Although filmmakers and protagonists might agree beforehand as to what themes or questions are "off-topic", in most cases the filmmaker would retain control over the nuances of the interview settings and use of the answers.

I claim that it is the interview form's seemingly objective and authentic character, which makes use of interviews an effective tool for authorial manipulation. It is therefore necessary to critically examine the dialectic between the interview and the role it plays in the film's aesthetic.

Nichols notes that 'the interview testifies to a power relation in which institutional hierarchy and regulation pertain to speech itself' (ibid., p. 50) and points to the origins of the cinematic interview in other fields:

> In medicine, it goes by the name of "case history," where patient-generated narratives of symptoms and their possible source become rewritten in the discourse of medical science. In anthropology, the interview is the testimony of native informants who describe the working of their culture to the one who will rewrite their accounts into the discourse of anthropological investigations. [...] in police work, the interrogation [...] in law, we find depositions, hearings, testimony, and cross-examination [...] In each case, hierarchy is maintained and served while information passes from one social agent to another. (p. 51)

In all these examples, the disparity in power between interviewer and interviewee is also a manifestation of the differences between theoretical, abstract knowledge and practical, concrete experiences – the doctor knows the history of the disease while the patient experiences the symptoms, the anthropologist masters the academic knowledge of foreign cultures while her informer is living them. I argue that when viewed in such a way, the power structure becomes more dialectic: the interviewer's theoretical knowledge (in the case of a filmmaker, her knowledge of filmmaking and her vision for her film) is incomplete without the concrete information given by the interviewee (the arguments, statements and stories needed for the edit). The filmmaker *needs* the protagonist's input. Still, she retains the power to do with it as she pleases. This is a further point to consider while examining documentary interviews.

Jay Ruby also points to the importance of form and the way authorial power is used to present interviews. He notes that the use of interviews and people's direct speech recognizes that the opinions of the experts and the vision of the filmmakers need to be tempered by the lived experience of the subjects and their view of themselves. It is "speaking with" instead of "speaking for." However, editorial control still remains in the hands of the filmmaker. The empowerment of the subject is therefore more illusionary than actual. While new voices are heard, traditional forms of authorship have not been significantly altered. (1991, p. 54)

The critical analysis of the interview form as a form of inherent inequity and power imbalance is crucial for the examination of documentaries. Certainly, some collaborative approaches, aesthetic devices and variations in form might slightly shift this inequity: a collaborative film in which the protagonist has an equal say in the editing process, such as *Limbo* discussed in Chapter 4.3, or reflexive elements making the audience conscious of how the interviews were cinematically manipulated. But I argue that the interview is an important manifestation of the power structures of the filmmaking process, and by examining it as such – positioning it critically in relation to the film's dramaturgic structure, the conditions engulfing its production or the filmmaker's overall position and partisanship – much can be learned regarding the film's political content and the way power structures are manifested in it.

Interviews in my practical work

Interviews play an important role in both my films, as both are pertaining to events either in the past, such as the killing of the Kilani family, or abstract and continuous in nature, such as Palestinian resistance and the concept of solidarity. As mentioned in Chapter 4.3, I attempted different forms of interview in ETLB and ultimately decided that the "talking head" form best served the aims of the film, giving the audience a more unmediated sense of being there and listening directly to the protagonists.

In one scene in the film, however, I utilized the "masked interview" form. In this scene at 52:10, the main protagonist, Ben, is seen discussing together with Palestinian activists the protests in the village and the potential of them advocating the idea of a "one-state-solution", referring to the idea of abolishing the current state apparatuses in the country and creating one democratic state for both Palestinians and Israelis in the entire area of mandatory Palestine pre-1948. I was filming a different scene when Ben, knowing that this topic was important to my film, came and whispered in my ear, informing me that such a discussion was taking place. I followed him with the camera as he sat down and began asking the other activists questions which he knew I was interested in filming. In the final film, the scene seems like a friendly and humorous conversation

Film Still 14: A "masked interview" situation in "Even Though My Land is Burning"

between comrades and provided me with some of the most important political statements of the film. There is no way for the audience to know that Ben was steering the conversation in the direction he knew I would like it to go.

This scene is a good example of the intricacy of the "masked interview". The question can at least be asked, in relation to form, whether this was an unfair manipulation of the activists participating in the scene. However, I offer it as an example of the possibilities for a more collaborative way of working, in which the protagonists are aware of and share the filmmaker's vision. Ben knew that the film's political positions and focus were similar to his own and supported me in getting the best footage to support those arguments, which I in turn could present in a more natural and authentic manner than would be the case with a formal interview.

In *Not Just Your Picture,* Paq and I opted at first for a combination of "talking head" interviews and conversation scenes, in which one or both of us are seen discussing with the protagonists in-frame (most such scenes were shot with two cameras, making it easier for us to turn the camera on each other or discuss while the other was filming). This approach proved valuable in getting the siblings to open up and in attaining more free, natural and authentic exchanges. Those scenes were usually not spontaneous: Paq and I planned to discuss a certain topic and instigated the conversation. But the shooting form allowed for more flexibility, especially for the protagonists, who were not constrained by the

Film Still 15: Ramsis Kilani and me in a conversation scene in "Not Just Your Picture" (not featured in the final version).

formal necessities of sitting in one spot to remain in-frame. While the shots in which we are clearly visible in the frame ended up not being used in the final cut as the film's visual style crystalized through the editing process, this approach supplied us with some of the most intimate moments of the film, such as when Ramsis bitterly reflects on the difficulties of pursuing a seemingly pointless legal struggle.

3.5 'You are looking at us like insects' – camera, sequence and the filmmaker's gaze

After considering and analysing how broader aesthetic means such as dramaturgy and narrative can be deconstructed to reveal the political power structures manifested in them, it is important to examine how these are manifested in the smallest building blocks of cinematic grammar as well – the shot and the sequence. I use the term sequence here to define the editing together of shots in a scene to create cinematic meaning and context.

One concept useful for this aim is the "Gaze". The concept of the Gaze and of looking as part of a subject/object dialectic or as a means of control and power is often discussed in the fields of psychoanalysis, such as in Jacques Lacan's theories of the "mirror stage" (cf. Lacan 2006), and sociology, as by Michel Foucault and his studies of prisons and the Panopticon (cf. 1991). It has been most prominently introduced into film studies by Laura Mulvey, who used psychoanalysis as her point of departure to articulate the male gaze as an element of a subject/object dichotomy between men and women, in which men are the ones actively looking while women are passively looked at (cf. 1989).

Paula Rabinowitz examines such question of the Gaze in documentary studies (1994). She creates a synthesis of the Freudian understanding of looking and voyeurism with Lukács's theories of proletarian epistemology (cf. Lukács 1971) and argues that 'the scene of class domination is the same as the scene of voyeurism, both depending on an (unspoken) desire of the object of the bourgeois subject's knowledge repossessing her power in difference' (1994, p. 36). She sets the questions of image-making and looking in a historical-political context:

> That the invention of photography coincides with the rise of commodity culture and serves as evidence of it, Walter Benjamin, the most astute theorist of photography, has made clear. Like the commodity itself, and the woman within commodity culture, photography's contribution to fabricating a society of the spectacle is dual – photographs are themselves objects of the gaze as well as purveyors of images [...] The photographic image reinforces bourgeois culture even when it seeks to expose its damaging effects as in the case of documentary photographs that reveal 'How the Other Half Lives'. Yet those objects – the classed, sexed, and gendered bodies of visual imagery – have the power to hold the gaze of their viewers; they are produced by *and* produce the 'political unconsciousness' of middle-class culture. (ibid., p. 37)

Rabinowitz defines the act of looking – and of being looked at – as political in itself, as embodying power relations of class and gender, regardless of the looker's intentions. The act of making images is therefore always located in a site imbued with power imbalances and class contradictions: 'Because it distinguishes observer from observed, yet brings the two into intimate contact, the photograph embodies this contradiction but seems unable to enter the realm of political effectivity' (p. 36).

For Rabinowitz this problem is an issue of reification. Reification is a form of human alienation under capitalism which makes subjective social relations seem objective and material (such as when the worker's social, lived labour put into producing a commodity appears as the commodity's inherent and objective natural value) and material objects seem subjective and social (such as when a commodity is ascribed, through exchange, value beyond its material function). This reification is part of the working class's alienation under capitalism, being itself reduced to a commodity – labour power – while also alienated from the fruits of its own work, from which it does not benefit. Rabinowitz draws on Lukács to claim that this is an epistemological issue, a question of how the exploited see and understand themselves:

For Lukács, class consciousness within the proletariat is dependent on the working class's ability to *see* itself as object and subject simultaneously. Reification produces a 'doubling of personality [...] splitting up of men into an element of the movement of commodities and an (objective and impotent) *observer* of that movement'. (p. 38)

Another concept pertaining to the act of looking in the encounter between filmmaker and protagonist is the 'return of the gaze' or 'visual riposte' articulated by Paula Amad (2013). Amad examines the possible political readings of a protagonist's look at the camera:

> I employ the phrase "return of the gaze" in a twofold manner. It refers to evidence of the look at the camera [...] by filmed subjects, and more generally it connotes the now-common interpretation of that look as a refusal of the assumed monolithic, unidirectionality of the West's technologically mediated structures of looking at cultural Others. There is therefore a difference in these two deployments of the term, the first referring more to the neutral evidence of subjects looking at the camera, and the second focusing on the now-conventional politicized interpretation of that look as a sort of unmediated and quasi-intentional address to the spectator. (p. 53)

Amad therefore questions whether a protagonist's look into the camera can be seen as resisting the power of the filmmaker's gaze: 'The hermeneutic of visual riposte is usually aroused by unintended, momentary evidence in the filmic text—when people look back at or toward the camera—that purportedly has the effect of unbalancing cinema's dominant gaze' (ibid.). This is an important point, since protagonists looking into the camera is common in documentary – including in my own practical work– and can be examined as part of a hermeneutic study of the film. It is therefore important to understand that such cinematic moments do not have a singular meaning and must be studied contextually and dialectically.

To exemplify these approaches, I examine three documentaries originating from different decades and filmed in different continents, which all share some common traits. First, while their overall dramaturgy differs in the use of means such as narration, the camera work in all of them can be characterized as observational. Second, they have all been made by white European filmmakers and depict non-white people, who face oppression under racist, colonial, and capitalist power structures.

The filmmakers' intent and motivation in making these films differ from one another, and I argue that this divergence in intent and motivation is manifested in the camera work and sequence editing. The films are *Workingman's Death* (Michael Glawogger, Austria/Germany 2005), *Les Maîtres Fous* (Jean Rouch, France 1955), and *Black Panthers* (Agnes Varda, France/US 1968).

"Workingman's Death"

Workingman's Death was produced by the respectively Austrian and German film production companies Lotus Film and the Quine Film, with funding from Austrian and German film funds and the broadcasters Arte and ORF. It has a runtime of 122 minutes and is defined on Lotus Film's website as follows:

> Is heavy manual labor disappearing or is it just becoming invisible? Where can we still find it in the 21st century?
> Workingman's Death follows the trail of the heroes in the illegal mines of the Ukraine, sniffs out ghosts among the sulfur workers in Indonesia, finds itself face to face with lions at a slaughterhouse in Nigeria, mingles with brothers as they cut a huge oil tanker into pieces in Pakistan, and joins Chinese steel workers in hopes of a glorious future. Meanwhile, the future is now in Germany, where a major smelting plant of bygone days has been converted into a bright and shiny leisure park. (Lotus Film 2018)

Workingman's Death is an impressive example of the technical possibilities of modern documentary cinematography, due in large part to the work of cinematographer Wolfgang Thaler. Filmed in unhospitable locations and physical conditions, it is composed of six chapters (or rather five chapters and an epilogue) depicting the state of workers in different parts of the world. The second chapter, *Ghosts*, which follows sulphur carriers in the Ijen volcano in Indonesia, is an interesting example of the documentary gaze.

The chapter starts at 31:10 with shots of fumes coming out of lit cracks in the ground, immediately deploying an aesthetic more commonly exhibited in horror movies which contrasts with the imagery of the first chapter, *Heroes*, filmed in the Donbass region. Those shots are sequenced together with the chants of a Muslim prayer, leading up to shots of the source of the sound – a ceremonial slaughtering of a goat. The following sequences from 33:10 are reminiscent of fiction film aesthetics: wide shots of smoke-filled landscapes and lines of workers making their way through them, framed at times as silhouettes against the skyline, similar to scenes in works of fiction such as *Lord of the Rings* (Jackson, NZ/US 2001, 2002, 2003) or *Game of Thrones* (Benioff and Weiss, US 2011–2019) or their precursors such as the works of Sergei Eisenstein or Andrei Tarkovsky.

This aesthetic continues throughout the chapter and is a central element of its cinematography. The images are supported by the heavily edited sound design of Paul Oberle, a rhythmic repetition of diegetic sounds. The chapter follows the sulphur carriers in their daily work, going up the mountain with empty baskets and returning carrying baskets full of chunks of sulphur weighing at times more than a hundred kilograms. From 34:15, the carriers' route is depicted mostly using a Steadicam in close proximity to the workers, a technique also more common in fictional cinematography.[30] Shots from the walk are intercut with observational scenes of workers conversing, one of them at 34:48 a short direct-address interview, which is made to fit the overall aesthetic by using a Steadicam tracking around the worker.

Much attention is paid to the materiality of the scene, using close-ups of the fumes, the baskets on the workers' shoulders or the chunks of sulphur. This attention to details conveys a strong sense of "being there", but also suggests a fascination with the visual aspects of poverty. In this context, it is instructive to look at Brian Winston's remarks on the documentaries of the Griersonian movement which

> usually concentrates on surfaces, even while managing to run from the social meaning of those surfaces [...] Given the aesthetic preferences of these film-makers, camera and editing style always tended to mannered composition and baroque image flow. This meant a tendency to seek the picturesque topic, but the search for the picturesque is to be found in even the least "aesthetic" subjects. Smoke damage in the *The Smoke Menace* (1937) looks as if it has been photographed by a prizewinner in a local photographic club competition [...] the slums are nearly always photographed in elegant compositions. (2008, p. 43)

Winston describes such an approach as making industrial locations into 'a site of high-contrast drama between light and shade, not a place of hazard and alienation' (ibid., p. 44).

I argue that *Workingman's Death* can indeed be seen as a continuation of the aesthetic of the Griersonian movement. This can be exemplified by comparing it with *The Song of Ceylon* (Basil Wright, UK 1934), produced by Grierson for the Ceylon Tea Propaganda Board and briefly discussed in Chapter 3. The shots in Wright's film are also carefully composed in a way closer to fiction and to art film than is typically the case for documentary film, making it 'one of the accepted masterpieces of documentary [...] remarkable in being so fully and freely a work of art' (McLane 2012, p. 81). The panning camera shots over long rows of tea workers climbing up a at 3:40, with its repetitive sound design, formalistic landscape shots and focus on the movements and details of the workers' actions are very similar to *Workingman's Death*.

This aestheticizing of the sulphur carriers' working conditions in *Workingman's Death* is an example of Rabinowitz's notes on reification explained above, as well as

---

30 Such aesthetic is recently gaining prominence in documentary films as well, mainly due to the development of light-weight cameras and affordable stabilizing systems such as the Gimbal, not available at the time of the film's production.

of Winston's comments on the social meaning of the Griersonian documentaries. The workers become things, much like actors in a Hollywoodesque spectacle which ignores all context and social conditions. When they do get a chance to speak, most of the dialogue is about drinking, having sex, getting into brawls and listening to Western music – with some short sentences regarding how they got to this line of work, sentences which play a small role in the overall dramaturgy.

From minute 48:00, during the workers' descent from the mountain, they encounter groups of tourists taking photos of each other, of the landscape and, at some point, of the workers themselves. These scenes are located in a way which draws our attention to the observational or voyeuristic aspects of the film and can be read as a reflexive analogy to the making of the film itself. At 48:55 we see German-speaking tourists interact with one of the workers, discussing among themselves how much they should pay for a souvenir, a possible reference to Glawogger's own home country of Austria and to the film's German and Austrian funding.

Such scenes are an example for Amad's concept of returning the gaze (2013) – they do not tackle the issue of the politics and power of the gaze embodied in Glawogger's physical act of observing, since the tourists act as a surrogate: it is their cameras being looked back at, not Glawogger's, who insists on maintaining the fourth-wall illusion of the scene. While this line of analysis alone does not permit a thorough examination of the power structures manifested in these scenes, it does provide an example of how such semi-reflexive elements can be used to draw the viewer's attention to other scenes exhibiting power imbalances, veiling the filmmaker's own power positionality.

In this sense, *Workingman's Death* is illustrative of Rabinowitz's view of voyeuristic observation as a site of class domination. The film was shot on 35 mm, requiring heavy equipment and making the encounter between the film team and protagonist a site of class imbalance in a very concrete way – poor workers carrying heavy baskets followed around by a European film team carrying a heavy camera, one side observing and the other being observed.

Workingman's Death is exemplary since it also points to a relation existing between highly stylized films – which often depend upon large budgets – and issues of political representation and position. This is what Espinosa sees as a question of "perfect" or "imperfect" cinema, discussed in Chapter 3:

> Imperfect cinema is no longer interested in quality or technique. It can be created equally well with a Mitchell or with an 8mm camera, in a studio or in a guerrilla camp in the middle of the jungle. Imperfect cinema is no longer interested in predetermined taste, and much less in "good taste." [...] The only thing it is interested in is how an artist responds to the following question: What are you doing in order to overcome the barrier

of the "cultured" elite audience which up to now has conditioned the form of your work? (1979, p. 26)

In such a way, Glawogger's gaze aestheticizes and "perfects" the exploitation of the sulphur carriers under global capitalism, exemplifying how the site of observing and being observed – separated by the divide of the means of film production – embodies the class contradictions analysed above by Rabinowitz.

"Les Maîtres Fous"

Jean Rouch's *Les Maîtres Fous* (1955), a 36-minutes ethnographic film, is part of Rouch's anthropological work in Africa. It was screened in the Venice Biennale and the Florence Film Festival and was banned from being screened by the British colonial administration in Ghana in 1955 due to its mocking of the colonial order (Reddy, n.d., sec. 4 par. 4). The website of the American distribution company Icarus Films describes the film as follows:

> THE MAD MASTERS (LES MAITRES FOUS), the most controversial and also the most widely celebrated work by ethnographic filmmaker Jean Rouch, depicts a possession ritual of the *Hauka* religious sect using the delirious techniques of "cine-trance." (Icarus Films 2018)

Les Maîtres Fous provides another example of a documentary film observing "the Other". Rouch is a French anthropologist and filmmaker, and as such his films serve different aims and use different methodologies to those of filmmakers such as Glawogger. This fact should not detract from the aesthetic and cinematic merits of his films, but should be taken into consideration when discussing them, as well as the five decades difference between them.

Les Maîtres Fous starts with an observational introduction of the living conditions in Accra, Ghana, narrated by the filmmaker. Five minutes in, its main subject matter is introduced – a trance-like ceremony of the Hauka movement, in which the participants mimic the roles of their colonial masters. Some of the first shots also have a certain similarity to an aesthetic commonly associated with fiction and horror film – at 5:00' we see a participant filmed from below, at a near-dusk hour, lit by a lamp mounted on the camera.

That's where the allusion to fictional aesthetic means seems to end. The beginning of the ceremony is filmed mostly from the side using a longer lens, panning with the participants' movement as they slowly enter a trance. At 13:35 we see a strong "return of the gaze" shot, as the 'corporal of the guard' stands up and looks firmly in the camera. The shot acknowledges the filmmakers' presence while the man's stern look hints at the possibility that he sees the film team or the white filmmaker as associated with the colonial masters.

As Amad argues above, this return of the gaze caught on film does not change the fact that Rouch holds the power position granted to him through control over the means of film production and possessing authorial ownership, but it does create a jarring effect, breaking the fourth wall and reminding the audience of the filmmaker's presence as well as the audience's own role in the colonial equation. Unlike the workers looking at the tourists in *Workingman's Death*, this return of the gaze serves as a reflexive alienating effect, reminding the European audience not only of the film being a film, but of their role in the colonial equation as well.

As the trance intensifies around 15:00, Rouch's camera seems to wander closer into the events. It retains a certain distance but allows us a closer look. The cinematography, while still also focusing on structures and materials, does so in a much more matter-of-fact manner and does not stylize the events – as one might also expect from an anthropological observation.

At 17:42 the film cuts to a different ceremony – drills of the colonial soldiers who we just watched being mimicked by the Hauka. The film ends with medium shots and close-ups of the participants in their daily lives as workers, starting at 26:18, smiling and looking at the camera. This now different return of the gaze hints at their acceptance of Rouch documenting their doings and depicts them as ordinary people, in contrast to their roles in the trance of the ceremony. Those shots humanize and individualize them, so that the audience can now view them as real people and not merely as colonial subjects or "mad" participants in a primitive ritual, and in doing so contextualizes the ceremony socially and politically.

Comparing *Les Maîtres Fous* with *Workingman's Death* serves as a further example for Rabinowitz's theory that observation entails a dichotomy of power between the observer and observed, and shows how important questions of aestheticizing, of *how* one is observed, are to the understanding of the political content of a film. By not over-stylizing the scene and implementing moments of "return of the Gaze", Rouch's camerawork is much more careful of the observer-observed dichotomy and the power inherent in the act of looking. It is a politically conscious film, which, while not dismantling the power structures inherent in it, manages to observe and document a highly complex subject matter while acknowledging the filmmaker's and the potential audience's own political position of power in relation to the protagonists as part of the broader power structures of colonialism. This has to do with Rouch's understanding of the role of the camera as an anthropological tool:

> My camera is not passive. The camera, from my point of view, is a kind of provocation. The provocation can be good or bad ... filming possession ceremonies like in *Les Maîtres fous* in some ways was dangerous because it was a very important ritual. If

something had gone wrong, I would have been responsible ... because I was there and had provoked it. (in Naficy 2007, p. 107)

It is in this context of Rouch's approach of that the camerawork of Les Maîtres fous should be seen, an approach connected to his understanding of shared anthropology. Rouch mentions that the priests themselves wanted the camera to be used as a tool in the ceremony, in order to show the film to people and "shock them into possession" (ibid., p. 103). This certainly makes for a very different encounter between camera and protagonist than in films such as Workingman's Death.

It is important to note that not only was Les Maîtres fous banned by the colonial administration, it drew criticism from Africans as well, who saw it as conveying an exoticized and racist portrayal of Africans. Senegalese filmmaker Ousmane Sembéne, in a conversation with Rouch in 1965, famously accused him and Africanists in general by saying: 'you are looking at us like insects' (Prédal 1982, p. 78).

"Black Panthers"

Black Panthers (1968) by French director Agnes Varda is a 27-minutes short documentary, filmed during Varda's stay in California at the time. It was scheduled for airing on French television in 1968 but was cancelled – according to Varda, due to its political potential to re-awaken the student protests which took place across the country earlier in the year (Mauldin 2014, par. 8). Its DVD distributor Criterion describes it on its website:

> Agnès Varda turns her camera on an Oakland demonstration against the imprisonment of activist and Black Panthers cofounder Huey P. Newton. In addition to evincing Varda's fascination with her adopted surroundings and her empathy, this perceptive short is also a powerful political statement. (Criterion 2018a)

In the film, Varda provides an account of the emergence, daily work and current struggles and aims of the newly founded *Black Panthers Party for Self Defence*, an African-American radical left party who called upon black people in the US to practice their constitutional right to bear arms as part of a strategy of resistance against racist police brutality.

Varda's documentation of the organisation begins at a critical time for the Party, shortly after its leader, Huey Newton, was arrested on charges of allegedly killing a police officer. The "Free Huey" campaign which ensued is considered a turning point for the Party, as it mobilized masses of African-Americans as well as white and other non-white radicals under its banner, giving the Party nationwide and global attention. The primary success of the Party, together with the unique global political dynamic of 1967–1968, brought many internationalist leftists around the world, including Varda herself, to sympathize with the Panthers (Letort 2014, p. 3), a context which is relevant to the examination of the film.

After the opening intertitle and a camera pan showing the words 'Black is honest and beautiful' written on a wall at 0:09, the film begins at 0:18 with a sequence of observational close-ups, shot from afar using a telescopic lens, of African-American men, women and children attending a concert. This view is characteristic of much of the film's content, which gleans much of its footage from political rallies and gatherings of the organisation, where Varda often assumes the position of an onlooker. We are introduced to the situation through a narration in the filmmaker's voice, similar to the way Jean Rouch introduces us to Accra in *Les Maîtres Fous*: 'This is no picnic in Oakland, this is a political rally …' Varda tells us at 1:50.

At 1:59, the long lens pans with members of the Party marching in military drills. In this first sequence a certain visual tension is already discernible, one which I argue is intentional and serves to emphasize certain political points throughout the film: a tension between, on the one hand, the framing of Panthers engaging in marches and military drills, usually shot from afar in a symmetrical way and with more decisive pans, emphasizing their order and discipline, and on the other, the portraits of supporters and children attending the events, which are usually shot in tighter framing, bringing a heightened sense of intimacy and immediacy, often using less accurate pans and zooms.

This aspect of the camerawork visualizes for the audience the different political dialectics in the party's work, in this case the relationship between the party's militant aspects, its rigid structure and discipline, and its communal aspects, social work and outreach programmes. The editing together of those shots in a sequence serves to emphasize the importance of a political organisation's ability to tend to both these aspects.

The fact that the overall dramaturgy of the film is built on introducing those different dialectics of political and revolutionary organising becomes evident in the next scene starting at 3:10, as Varda changes to a different camera style, now filming the streets of Oakland from the window of a moving vehicle. After a few short shots of black children in Oakland, ending with a shot of one wearing a T-shirt with the word "Help" printed on it fiercely returning the gaze at 4:19, we return to the rally. This short excursion into the streets of Oakland again serves to visually connect the political base in the community with the vanguard party.

At 4:25, Varda visualises another dialectic she apparently sees as necessary to a revolutionary organisation, this time in-frame: a speech by one of the party's member is being filmed with another member standing guard in the foreground, framed in a tight close-up on the right while the speaker makes his speech in the background on the left. This is a further visualisation of the two aspects of the political work, the practical militancy on the one hand and the political theory and propaganda work on the other. Varda repeats this style of framing while filming speeches in later parts of the film as well, strengthening the claim that this is an intentional choice of camera positions.

Varda's political aims are made clear by the narration in her voice, but there are manifestations of them in the cinematography and editing as well. At 8:36, we see a speech by activist Stokely Carmichael, shot in a tight close-up from eye level. This framing would be uncommon in news reports and creates a strong feeling of trust and intimacy and a sense that Varda wishes to bring his words closer to her European audience. In general, there is much room being given in the film for the Party to present its agenda in its own words; for example Varda films members reading the party's ten-point-programme and places this scene prominently in the middle of the film at 11:50. I assert that this scene is meant to show an example of revolutionary dialectic, again by stressing the connection between the party's theoretical programme and its practical work.

The film ends with a sequence of shots of the walls of the party's Oakland headquarters at 25:50, now ridden with bullet holes after local police had opened fire on the building, ending with a close-up of Huey Newton's iconic poster hanging behind the broken window. Newton, dressed in the Party's uniform of black leather jacket and beret, is holding a gun and a spear, sitting on an African wicker chair and looking at the camera. This too creates a "return of the gaze" effect, albeit once removed, as Varda is filming a poster made by the Party, while Newton himself is in Jail. Although Varda thus creates the effect of Newton looking directly at the audience, it is a different "return of the gaze" since Newton was staring at his party's photographer and not at Varda. Nevertheless, it creates a similar alienation effect on the viewer, and serves as a reflexive device.

Varda's fascination with the party's radical politics and militancy has been criticized, and the film's aesthetic taken as an example of Varda being 'blind to the political impact of an imagery that tapped into archetypal fantasies' (Letort 2014, p. 4) and 'reviving racist stereotypes of blackness' (ibid.). Such criticism interprets the imagery as perhaps white Americans might have, instead of attempting to understand the emancipatory and mobilizing potential of the Panthers' self-representation, and its depiction by Varda. Beth Mauldin, on the other hand, finds that the film 'captures the complexity of the party, with its blend of personal, domestic and international politic' (2014). I claim that it is evident from the film's aesthetic that Varda is presenting the Black Panthers the way she thought they would like to be represented, as a partisan, political filmmaker who does not hide her sympathy with her protagonists but rather tries to apply her own political analysis to their activities, in order to document, analyse and make them accessible to other activists around the world, thereby doing her part to support what she sees as their struggle against exploitation and oppression.

Black Panthers poses a third example of the politics of the act of looking. It tries to make the encounter between the observer and the observed actively political – one of exchange rather than oppression. Still, this encounter remains unidirectional, but the way in which Varda's unabashed partisanship is evident in the aesthetics further exemplifies the possibilities of examining such aesthetics for manifestations of power and political positions.

Politics of the gaze in my own practical work

The camera's position and perspective are important narrative device in my own work, one which also carries political meaning. *Even Though My Land is Burning* takes place in a village which is a hot-spot for journalists and TV crews from all over the world, there have therefore been plenty of reportages and video reports on Nabi Saleh and, as is also discussed in the film, much of this work is conducted by the villagers themselves. It was therefore important for me to create a film which is also artistic and analytic, and not a mere video report. In order to emphasize this being a film and not a report, I looked for poetic approaches to filming which would avoid an over-aestheticizing of the reality.

Some aspects of the camerawork were predetermined by the circumstances. Constrictions of budget comprised one such constraint, but mostly my wish to not stand out from the crowd and to maintain the possibility of being seen and accepted as a protestor and not a journalist, meant filming with a small DSLR camera without a tripod. This condition determined a certain style beforehand and ruled out some aesthetic options altogether – the gliding movements of a Steadicam or a stabilizer or the fluid pans of a good heavy tripod.

My decisions regarding the perspective of the film – to tell the story through Ben's eyes, as well as to engage in solidary dialogue with the activists –significantly influenced the camera style. This meant, for example, that I would never film the events from the side of the soldiers: although it might have been possible for me to present myself as a journalist, discuss with the soldiers in Hebrew and claim to be a neutral observer in order to be able to have more freedom of movement, this was never entertained as an option. For that reason, the protest scenes are all filmed from within or behind the protestors. This resulted in the over-the-shoulder shot being a reoccurring aesthetic throughout the film. This

Film Still 16: Scene from "Even Though My Land is Burning"

was a style I maintained while following Ben in less intense moments of the film as well, in moments where he was talking to other activists or simply resting, in order to tell the story through his eyes by literally bringing the camera perspective as close to his as possible.

Such aesthetic decisions resulted in several poetic and metaphorical approaches to the cinematography, for example when Ben is filmed from the back looking at the hills surrounding the village, placing him in relation to the land and alluding to the main theme of the film: the question of the country being "his", "theirs" or belonging to all.

In order to emphasize my position as a filmmaker, I focused on the experiences of being part of the demonstration from my perspective as well. One way in which this was done was by keeping the camera running in moments of running away from the military or from tear-gas grenades. This acted as a reflexive device, showing the audience that I as a filmmaker was not shielded from the violence of the scene.

Another theme of the film is the question and definition of violence during the demos. It is very common for the village's youth to throw stones at the advancing military, an act they see as legitimate resistance. As discussed in a previous chapter, this is an issue that was thematised in the interviews with Bassem, Manal and Ben, but was important for me to address visually as well. One of my first thoughts while researching for the film was to get hold of a camera capable

Film Still 17: Ben Ronen in the village of Nabi Saleh

of good high framerate recordings and a gas mask, and to shoot stylized slow-motion shots of demonstrators hurling stones through clouds of tear-gas. While shooting the film, however, I realized that this approach would be too aestheticizing, creating a fiction-like style, in a way similar to the scenes discussed before in *Workingman's Death*. Being inside the tear-gas clouds would further suggest a privileged camera position unscathed by the risks on the ground, which would go against my original visual concept.

I decided not to film those shots and opted for a simpler solution, one which also stressed my own position, physically and narratively. I filmed many shots of youth throwing stones using a long lens while positioning myself further away, out of harm's reach. I then edited those shots in sequences with music and heavy sound design in order to present them in a more dramatic and poetic way, but still as "normal" shots, without the alienating effects of slow-motion. In this way, it becomes apparent to the audience that those shots were filmed by someone taking part in the protests themselves.

One scene which exemplifies this approach is a long take of masked youth throwing rocks at a "skunk" truck off screen at 54:53.[31] The only elements making

---

31 "Skunk" is a bio-organic mixture used by the Israeli military against protestors, basically consisting of a water cannon shooting sewage-like smelling liquid which is almost impossible to remove from cloths or skin.

Film Still 18: Youth throwing rocks at a military "skunk" truck in "Even Though My Land is Burning"

the "skunk's" presence known is the sound of its motor and the liquid pouring down from the top of the frame. Since this scene comes at a point in the film in which I wanted to emphasize Ben's pessimism and the toll the protests have taken on him, I superimposed it with a dreary song by Ben's punk-rock Band "Marmara Streisand" who are featured in the film's epilogue. The shot of masked youth throwing rocks at an unseen threat, a deliberate allusion to the imagery of David and Goliath, together with the song's hard style and dark lyrics on feelings of imprisonment and isolation provided a poetic metaphor which fitted the dramaturgic needs of the scene.

In this way, I often tried to create images which worked metaphorically as well as informatively. One example at 37:05 shows Ben playing with Samer, Manal's young son. I was sitting on the couch on the other side of the room as the two picked up some of the many used and empty tear-gas canister on the coffee table, common in the homes of the village, and started playing with them, looking through them as though they were telescopes. At some point, they brought the two together, looking at each other through one long tube resembling a camera lens. This image of an Israeli activist and a Palestinian child, trying to see and frame each other using the remains of used Israeli weapons with a textured wall between them, further articulated my political position and the subtext of my film through observational shots, in a way I considered respectful to the protagonists and portrays them as they would like to portray themselves.

Film Still 19: Ben Ronen and Samer Tamimi in "Even Though My Land is Burning"

For *Not Just Your Picture*, Anne Paq and I also conceptualized an intimate and immediate film, which would not hide our own physical and political positions in relation to the protagonists. This meant that the technical method of shooting was quite similar to *ETLB* – we shot with two small DSLR cameras, often hand-held, and attempted to be as close to the protagonists as possible.

A major difference between *NJYP* and *ETLB* is the fact that the chaos, stress and dynamic of the demonstrations in Nabi Saleh meant I could be "forgotten" by the protagonists, who were often busy concentrating on their own safety. In *NJYP*, mostly shot in the protagonists' homes or daily lives, the presence of the camera was more imposing. To achieve the authenticity we wanted, we had to go through a process of making the protagonists feel at ease with the cameras. This process proved successful, when Ramsis himself once noted to us that he found it much easier to 'forget the camera' as the production progressed.

Especially while filming in the siblings' hometown Siegen, we usually had our cameras with us throughout the day and could pick them up and film whenever a situation presented itself. In this way, we were able to catch many interesting glimpses of the siblings' daily lives. As mentioned in section 4.4, in most of those scenes we were two filmmakers using two cameras, and this enabled us to capture discussions between us and the protagonists better, as one of us was always able to film while the other was talking. This had an effect on the dynamic between us and the protagonists, making us more accessible and able

Film Still 20: Ramsis and Layla Kilani in Layla's bedroom in "Not Just Your Picture"

to engage in real conversation, and eased the observer-observed dichotomy by allowing space for discussion while communicating to the protagonists that we were always willing to turn off the cameras.

One "return of the gaze" moment is built into the film as well, in the scene in which Ramsis talks about his despair from the legal struggle. As he states that such a struggle would take years and become his whole life, he stares tiredly into the lens, thus looking the audience direct in the eye, a moment which helps the scene fulfil its role in making the difficulties of his quest for justice more palatable to the viewer.

4. Conclusion

Images and narrative representations of "the real" are all around us, in newspapers, TV, commercials and cinemas. They draw their subject matter from reality and in turn, shape the way we view this reality, the way we interact with it and consequently, affect it. Studying the way reality is represented is in no way an abstract philosophical endeavour, but one which is relevant to many concrete aspects of our lives.

In this research, I examined the aesthetic and cinematic manifestations of the power structures between filmmaker and protagonists in documentary film, aiming to explore the different interrelations between social structures and documentary. This is a topic I believe is often not addressed enough in documentary scholarship, and by using case studies, presenting different theories and approaches and relying on my own practical experiences as filmmaker I suggested new ways for the political reading of documentaries.

Although I have concentrated on the field of documentary film, the core of my research is applicable to many other fields as well. If Marxist theories has taught me anything, it is that under capitalism nothing is quite the way it appears, and that behind any "thing" lies an intricate web of social relations, material conditions and political and economic interests. Such understanding is crucial for our dealing with and scholarship of film and visual culture.

As discussed in this book, the social conditions affecting the field of documentary are ever-evolving. Easier access to means of production through cheaper equipment or crowdfunding allows more people to create documentaries, while neo-liberal production and distribution paradigms under late capitalism cause incremental but steady changes in the ways that films are promoted and perceived. While they can be positive or negative, such changes mean that we must constantly look for new ways to analyse and study documentary film, as well as for new applications of known and existing methods.

I assert that the theoretical frameworks of dialectical materialism and hermeneutics I present in this paper are key tools for conducting such analysis and study. Just as our media landscape is ever-changing, so must be our tools of critiquing it, and there is much gain to be made by using such approaches, which take into consideration the myriad elements influencing a documentary, from its inception to its reception. In a society which is becoming more and more used to accepting things at face value, in which facts and science are reduced to mere opinions, such critical approaches become ever-more valuable.

Making my first steps as a lecturer while working on this research, I saw that young film students today are not only fully capable of understanding such seemingly complex themes and integrating them into their work, but that they are themselves motivated and curious to do so. I believe that understanding the power the camera gives us as filmmakers is just as important for a young student as learning the importance of a cutaway or a smooth camera pan, perhaps even more so, and I therefore hope that colleagues might also be able to integrate some of this research into their teaching.

I sincerely hope that this paper will also prove to be a useful practical tool for filmmakers, regardless of whether they see themselves as "political filmmakers" or – even better – understand that all films are political. I hope that by sharing my experiences and my insights I have been able to make the case for a stronger connection between the practice and theory of documentary filmmaking, both in the academy and on set. I know that the time I spent researching has changed my view of both immensely, and I hope it might have a similar transformative potential on those who read it.

List of film stills

Film Still 1:	Ahed Tamimi in "Even Though My Land is Burning"	36
Film Still 2:	Ben Ronen and Manal Tamimi in "Even Though My Land is Burning"	38
Film Still 3:	Layla Kilani holds a photo of her father Ibrahim and herself in "Not Just Your Picture"	39
Film Still 4:	Layla and Ramsis Kilani watching home videos of their father in "Not Just Your Picture"	42
Film Still 5:	Ibrahim's brother, Salah, holding pictures of Layla and Ramsis in the family's home in Gaza	66
Film Still 6:	Bassem Tamimi and Ben Ronen in Tamimi's home in "Even Though My Land is Burning"	67
Film Still 7:	An interview with Ben Ronen in "Even Though My Land is Burning"	87
Film Still 8:	Ben Ronen before a demonstration in "Even Though My Land is Burning"	88
Film Still 9:	Co-director Anne Paq in Ramallah showing Layla Kilani footage of her family in Gaza	90
Film Still 10:	Protagonist Reza and director Asal Akhavan in "Limbo"	91
Film Still 11:	Reza meeting NGO workers in "Limbo"	93
Film Still 12:	Reza addressing me behind the camera in "Limbo"	94
Film Still 13:	Director Asal Akhavan showing Reza footage in a scene from "Limbo"	95
Film Still 14:	A "masked interview" situation in "Even Though My Land is Burning"	108
Film Still 15:	Ramsis Kilani and me in a conversation scene in "Not Just Your Picture" (not featured in the final version).	109
Film Still 16:	Scene from "Even Though My Land is Burning"	121
Film Still 17:	Ben Ronen in the village of Nabi Saleh	122
Film Still 18:	Youth throwing rocks at a military "skunk" truck in "Even Though My Land is Burning"	123
Film Still 19:	Ben Ronen and Samer Tamimi in "Even Though My Land is Burning"	124
Film Still 20:	Ramsis and Layla Kilani in Layla's bedroom in "Not Just Your Picture"	125

List of films

August: A Moment Before the Eruption, 2002. Directed by: Avi Mograbi. Israel.
Between Fences, 2016. Directed by: Avi Mograbi. Israel.
Black Panthers, 1968. Directed by: Agnes Varda. US/France.
Chauka, Please Tell Us the Time, 2017. Directed by: Behrouz Boochani and Arash Servastani. Netherlands.
Class Divide, 2015. Directed by: Marc Levin. US.
Das Experiment, 2016. Produced by: Die Welt. Germany.
First Person, 2000. Directed by: Errol Morris. US.
Five Broken Cameras, 2011. Directed by: Emad Burnat and Guy Davidi. Palestine/Israel
Gaga: Five Foot Two, 2017. Directed by: Chris Moukarbel. US.
Gambling, Gods and LSD, 2004. Directed by: Peter Mettler. Canada.
Game of Thrones, 2011-. Produced by: David Benioff and D.B. Weiss. US.
Grey Gardens, 1975. Directed by: Albert and David Maysles. US.
Grizzly Man, 2005. Directed by: Werner Herzog. US.
Happy Birthday Mr. Mograbi, 1999. Directed by: Avi Mograbi. Israel.
Hoop Dreams, 1994. Directed by: Steve James and Frederick Marx. US.
Housing Problems, 1935. Directed by: Edgar Anstey and Arthur Elton. UK.
Hour of the Furnaces, 1968. Directed by: Octavio Getino and Fernando Solanas. Argentina.
How I Learned to Overcome My Fear and Love Arik Sharon, 1997. Directed by: Avi Mograbi. Israel.
Komsomol Patron of Electrification, 1932. Directed by: Esfir Shub. USSR.
Les Maîtres Fous, 1995. Directed by: Jean Rouch. France.
Limbo, 2012. Directed by: Asal Akhavan. Germany.
Live Nude Girls Unite!, 2000. Directed by: Vicki Funary and Julia Query. US.
Love Me, 2014. Directed by: Jonathon Narducci. US.
Man on Wire, 2008. Directed by: James Marsh. US.
Man with a Movie Camera, 1929. Directed by: Dziga Vertov. USSR.
Nanook of the North, 1922. Directed by: Robert Flaherty. US.
Nostalgia for the Light, 2011. Directed by: Patricio Guzmán. Chile.

Once I Entered a Garden, 2012. Directed by: Avi Mograbi. Israel.
#Obliterated Families, 2016. Produced by: Anne Paq and Ala Qandil. France/Poland.
Roger & Me, 1989. Directed by: Michael Moore. US.
Sarah Palin: You Betcha!, 2011. Directed by: Nick Broomfield. UK.
The Battle of Chile: Part I, 1975. Directed by: Patricio Guzmán. Chile.
The Battle of Chile: Part II, 1976. Directed by: Patricio Guzmán. Chile.
The Battle of Chile: Part III, 1979. Directed by: Patricio Guzmán. Chile.
The Fog of War: Eleven Lessons from the Life of Robert S. McNamara, 2004. Directed by: Errol Morris. US.
The King of Kong: A Fistful of Quarters, 2007. Directed by: Seth Gordon. US.
The Lord of the Rings: The Fellowship of the Ring, 2001. Directed by: Peter Jackson. New Zealand/US.
The Lord of the Rings: The Return of the King, 2003. Directed by: Peter Jackson. New Zealand/US.
The Lord of the Rings: The Two Towers, 2002. Directed by: Peter Jackson. New Zealand/US.
The Song of Ceylon, 1934. Directed by: Basil Wright. UK.
The Thin Blue Line, 1988. Directed by: Errol Morris. US.
The War Room, 1993. Directed by: D. A. Pennebaker and Chris Hegedus. US.
Three Songs for Lenin, 1933. Directed by: Dziga Vertov. USSR.
Welcome to Leith, 2015. Directed by: Michael Beach Nichols and Christopher Walker. US.
Workingman's Death, 2005. Directed by: Michael Glawogger. Austria/Germany.
Z32, 2008. Directed by: Avi Mograbi. Israel.

Bibliography

Adorno, T. W., 1958. *Einführung in die Dialektik*. Berlin: Suhrkamp.

A Foreign Affair, 2018. *A Foreign Affair's Media Directory*. loveme.com [online]. Available from: https://www.loveme.com/information/media.shtml [Accessed 15 Feb 2018].

Ahmad, M. Y.-A., Dessel, A. B., Mishkin, A., Ali, N., and Omar, H., 2015. Intergroup Dialogue as a Just Dialogue: Challenging and Preventing Normalization in Campus Dialogues. *Digest of Middle East Studies*, 24 (2), 236–259.

Akhavan, A., 2013. Limbo – A Shared Visual Anthropological Research with a Refugee in Berlin. Master's Thesis. Free University, Berlin.

Akrap, D., 2015. Germany's Response to the Refugee Crisis Is Admirable. But I Fear It Cannot Last | Opinion |. *The Guardian* [online]. Available from: https://www.theguardian.com/commentisfree/2015/sep/06/germany-refugee-crisis-syrian [Accessed 28 Mar 2018].

Alea, T. G., 1984. The Viewer's Dialectic, part. *Jump Cut*, (29), 18–21.

Amad, P., 2013. Visual Riposte: Looking Back at the Return of the Gaze as Postcolonial Theory's Gift to Film Studies. *Cinema Journal*, 52 (3), 49–74.

Assmann, J., 1999. *Das kulturelle Gedächtnis: Schrift, Erinnerung und politische Identität in frühen Hochkulturen*. Munich: C.H. Beck.

Azoulay, A., 2008. *The Civil Contract of Photography*. Cambridge, MA: MIT Press.

Azoulay, A., 2015. *Civil Imagination: A Political Ontology of Photography*. London: Verso.

Barclay, B., 2003. Celebrating Fourth Cinema. *Illusions*, (35), 7–11.

Barnouw, E., 1974. *Documentary: A History of the Non-Fiction Film*. Oxford: Oxford University Press.

Beach Nichols, M., 2018. Welcome to Leith – Feature Documentary. Kickstarter [online]. Available from: https://www.kickstarter.com/projects/903839421/welcome-to-leith-feature-documentary [Accessed 15 Feb 2018].

Beckett, L., 2017a. 'A White Girl Had to Die for People to Pay Attention': Heather Heyer's Mother on Hate in the US. *The Guardian* [online]. 1 October 2017. Available from: http://www.theguardian.com/us-news/2017/oct/01/heather-heyers-mother-on-hate-in-the-us-were-not-going-to-hug-it-out-but-we-can-listen-to-each-other [Accessed 15 Feb 2018].

Beckett, L., 2017b. How Leftwing Media Focus on Far-Right Groups Is Helping to Normalize Hate. *The Guardian* [online]. 5 March 2017. Available from: http://www.theguardian.com/world/2017/mar/05/left-wing-media-far-right-normalize-hate-trump [Accessed 15 Feb 2018].

Berg, A., 2016. 'Continue Doing Films Inspite and Next to the Despair' – Interview with Avi Mograbi Before the Premiere of 'Between Fences' in the Berlinale. *Spitz Magazine* [online], (20). Available from: http://spitzmag.de/culture/7513 [Accessed 26 Jan 2018].

Bosanquet, B. and Bryant, W. M., 1886. *Selections from Hegel's Lectures on Aesthetics. Part 3, Section 3* [online]. Available from: https://www.marxists.org/reference/archive/hegel/works/ae/part3-section3-chapter3.htm [Accessed 15 Feb 2018].

Bourdieu, P., 2005. *Questions de sociologie*. Tel-Aviv: Resling.

Boycott!, 2014. *Heartbeat is a normalization project that violates BNJYP guidelines*. Boycott! Supporting the Palestinian Boycott Call from Within [online]. Available from: http://boycottisrael.info/content/heartbeat-normalization-project-violates-bds-guidelines [Accessed 27 Apr 2019].

Brecht, B., 2007. Against Georg Lukács. In: *Aesthetics and Politics*. London: Verso.

Bruzzi, S., 2006. *New Documentary*. New York: Routledge.

Buckow, A., 2016. Boykott den Boykotteuren. *Jungle World* [online]. 3 March 2016. Available from: https://jungle.world/artikel/2016/09/boykott-den-boykotteuren [Accessed 1 Feb 2018].

Catliff, S. and Granville, J., 2013. *The Casting Handbook: For Film and Theatre Makers*. London: Routledge.

Chanan, M., 2007. *Politics of Documentary*. London: British Film Institute.

Chapman, J., 2009. *Issues in Contemporary Documentary*. Cambridge, UK: Polity Press.

Criterion, 2018a. *Black Panthers* [online]. The Criterion Collection. Available from: http://www.criterion.com/films/28627-black-panthers [Accessed 28 Mar 2018].

Criterion, 2018b. *Hoop Dreams (1994)* [online]. The Criterion Collection. Available from: https://www.criterion.com/films/906-hoop-dreams [Accessed 26 Apr 2018].

Cunningham, M., 2014. *The Art of Documentary*. San Francisco: New Riders.

Darweish, M. and Rigby, A., 2015. *Popular Protest in Palestine: The Uncertain Future of Unarmed Resistance*. London: Pluto Press.

Davis, K. C., 1999. White Filmmakers and Minority Subjects: Cinema Verite and the Politics of Irony in 'Hoop Dreams' and 'Paris Is Burning'. *South Atlantic Review*, 64 (1), 26.

Ebert, R., 2009. *The great American documentary.* Roger Ebert [online]. 5 November 2009. Available from: https://www.rogerebert.com/rogers-journal/the-great-american-documentary [Accessed 15 Feb 2018].

Eco, U., 1990. Interpretation and Overinterpretation: World, History, Texts. Presented at the The Tanner Lectures on Human Values, Cambridge, UK.

Eglash, R., 2018. 20 Groups that Advocate Boycotting Israel Will Now Be Denied Entry. *The Washington Post* [online], 2018. Available from: https://www.washingtonpost.com/news/worldviews/wp/2018/01/07/18-groups-that-advocate-boycotting-israel-will-now-be-denied-entry/ [Accessed 1 Oct 2018].

Espinosa, G., 1979. For An Imperfect Cinema. *Jump Cut*, (20), 24–26.

Even, A. and Tal, R., n.d. Interview with Avi Mograbi. תקריב כתב עת לקולנוע דוקומנטרי [online]. Available from: https://takriv.net/article/%d7%a8%d7%90%d7%99%d7%95%d7%9f-%d7%a2%d7%9d-%d7%90%d7%91%d7%99-%d7%9e%d7%95%d7%92%d7%a8%d7%91%d7%99/ [Accessed 27 Mar 2018].

Feroz, E., 2014. Mein Vater sagte, wir sollten uns nicht sorgen. *Die Presse* [online]. 28 July 2014. Available from: https://diepresse.com/home/politik/aussenpolitik/3845667/Mein-Vater-sagte-wir-sollten-uns-nicht-sorgen [Accessed 10 Jan 2018].

Feroz, E., 2015. The Forgotten Massacre of German Citizens in Gaza. *The Electronic Intifada* [online]. 7 August 2015. Available from: https://electronicintifada.net/content/forgotten-massacre-german-citizens-gaza/14754 [Accessed 10 Jan 2018].

Flakin, W., 2016. Antideutsche wollten kritische jüdische Stimmen zum Schweigen bringen. *Die Freiheitsliebe* [online]. 9 March 2016. Available from: https://diefreiheitsliebe.de/kultur/antideutsche-wollten-kritische-juedische-stimmen-zum-schweigen-bringen-im-gespraech-mit-dror-dayan/ [Accessed 1 Feb 2018].

Foucault, M., 1991. *Discipline and Punish: The Birth of a Prison.* London: Penguin.

Gadamer, H.-G., 2010. Wahrheit und Methode. *In: Gesammelte Werke.* Tübingen: Mohr Siebeck.

Garcia, A., 2018. *NCAA Surpasses $1 Billion in Revenue for First Time.* CNNMoney Sports [online]. Available from: https://money.cnn.

com/2018/03/07/news/companies/ncaa-revenue-billion/index.html [Accessed 27 Apr 2019].

Getino, O. and Solanas, F., 1969. Toward a Third Cinema. *Tricontinental*, (14), 107–132.

Gillard, G., 2009. *Film as Text* [online]. Available from: http://garrygillard.net/writing/filmastext.html [Accessed 27 Apr 2018].

Ginsburg, F., 1991. Indigenous Media: Faustian Contract or Global Village? *Cultural Anthropology*, 6 (1), 92–112.

Govaert, C., 2011. Cueing the Viewer. PhD. University of Aberdeen, Aberdeen, Scotland.

Gramsci, A., 1971. *Selection from the Prison Notebooks of Antonio Gramsci*. New York: International Publishers.

Gramsci, A., 1985. *Selections from Cultural Writings*. London: Lawrence and Wishart.

Grant, B. K. and Sloniowski, J., 1998. *Documenting the Documentary: Close Readings of Documentary Film and Video*. Detroit, MI: Wayne State University Press.

Greene, R., 2015. How to Create a Documentary Character | Unfiction. *Sight & Sound* [online]. 19 March 2015. Available from: http://www.bfi.org.uk/news-opinion/sight-sound-magazine/comment/unfiction/how-create-documentary-character [Accessed 19 Feb 2017].

Grierson, T., 2016. The Documentary That Went Inside the White Nationalist Movement Before Everyone Else. *MEL Magazine* [online]. 14 December 2016. Available from: https://melmagazine.com/the-documentary-that-went-inside-the-white-nationalist-movement-before-everyone-else-53037e1c5238 [Accessed 16 Jan 2018].

Grindon, L., 2007. Q&A: Poetics of the Documentary Film Interview. *The Velvet Light Trap*, 60 (1), 4–12.

Guerrasio, J., 2014. An Oral History of Hoop Dreams, 20 Years After Its Première. *The Dissolve* [online]. 15 January 2014. Available from: https://thedissolve.com/features/oral-history/360-an-oral-history-of-hoop-dreams-20-years-after-its-/ [Accessed 15 Feb 2018].

Gupta, S. H., 2015. Meet the 2015 Sundance Filmmakers #9: 'Welcome to Leith' Directors Tackle Extremism in Rural America. *IndieWire* [online]. 14 January 2015. Available from: http://www.indiewire.com/2015/01/meet-the-2015-sundance-filmmakers-9-welcome-to-leith-directors-tackle-extremism-in-rural-america-66277/ [Accessed 15 Feb 2018].

Hackett, R. A., 1985. A Hierarchy of Access: Aspects of Source Bias in Canadian TV News. *Journalism Quarterly*, 62 (2), 256–277.

Hall, S., 2011. The Neo-Liberal Revolution. *Cultural Studies*, 25 (6), 705–728.

Hass, A., 2010. Shin Bet Puts Israeli 'Anarchists' in Crosshairs. *Haaretz* [online]. 27 December 2010. Available from: https://www.haaretz.com/print-edition/features/shin-bet-puts-israeli-anarchists-in-crosshairs-1.333140 [Accessed 1 Oct 2018].

Hayano, D. M., 1979. Auto-Ethnography: Paradigms, Problems, and Prospects. *Human Organization*, 38 (1), 99–104.

Haymes, S., Vidal de Haymes, M., and Miller, R., eds., 2015. *The Routledge Handbook of Poverty in the United States*. London: Routledge.

Hegel, G. W. F., 1977. *Phenomenology of Spirit*. Wotton-under-edge: Clarendon Press.

Herreria, C., 2017. NYT Accused of Normalizing White Nationalism In 'Nazi Sympathizer' Profile. *HuffPost UK* [online]. 26 November 2017. Available from: http://www.huffingtonpost.com/entry/new-york-times-nazi-next-door-profile_us_5a19f05ce4b0d4906caf1e8b [Accessed 15 Feb 2018].

Hohenberger, E., 1992. Zwischen Zwei Filmen: Eklektisches Zur Deutschen Dokumentarfilmgeschichte Zwischen Von Wegen Schicksal (1979) Und Hätte Ich Mein Herz Sprechen Lassen ... (1990). *Frauen Und Film*, (52), 80–88.

Hood, S., 1983. John Grierson and the Documentary Film Movement. *In*: *British Cinema History*. London: Weidenfeld & Nicolson.

hooks, bell, 2009. *Reel to Real: Race, Class and Sex at the Movies*. New York: Routledge.

Hotline for Refugees and Migrants, 2016. 'Between Fences': Watch Avi Mograbi's Documentary on People Incarcerated in 'Holot'. *Hotline for Refugees and Migrants* [online]. Available from: https://hotline.org.il/%d7%a6%d7%a4%d7%95-%d7%91%d7%a1%d7%a8%d7%98-%d7%91%d7%99%d7%9f-%d7%92%d7%93%d7%a8%d7%95%d7%aa-%d7%a1%d7%a8%d7%98%d7%95-%d7%94%d7%aa%d7%99%d7%a-2%d7%95%d7%93%d7%99-%d7%a9%d7%9c-%d7%90%d7%91/ [Accessed 15 Feb 2018].

Icarus Films, 2018. *Icarus Films: The Mad Masters* [online]. Available from: http://icarusfilms.com/if-mf [Accessed 28 Mar 2018].

IMDb.com, 2018. *The King of Kong: A Fistful of Quarters (2007) - IMDb* [online]. Available from: https://www.imdb.com/title/tt0923752/ [Accessed 26 Apr 2018].

Jameson, F., 1971. The Case for Georg Lukács. *In*: *Marxism and Form: Twentieth-Century Dialectical Theories of Literature*. Princeton: Princeton University Press, 160–205.

Jeffries, S., 2012. Why Marxism Is on the Rise Again. *The Guardian* [online]. 7 April 2012. Available from: https://www.theguardian.com/world/2012/jul/04/the-return-of-marxism [Accessed 27 Apr 2019].

Jessop, B., 2012. Marxist Approaches to Power. In: *The Wiley-Blackwell Companion to Political Sociology*. Hoboken, NJ: John Wiley & Sons, Incorporated, 3–15.

Jhally, S., *Stuart Hall – Representation and the Media (video recording)*, 1997. Northampton, MA: Media Education Foundation.

Kadman, N., 2009. Rafah Crossing: Who Holds the Keys? Tel Aviv-Jaffa: Gisha-Legal Center for Freedom of Movement.

Kanafani, G., 2000. *Palestine's Children: Returning to Haifa and Other Stories*. 1st ed. Boulder, CO: Lynne Rienner Publishers.

Koutsourakis, A., 2015. Symptomatic Reading. In: *The Routledge Encyclopedia of Film Theory*. London: Routledge.

La Valle, D., 2014. Interview: Jonathan Narducci talks about Love Me. *Scene Creek* [online]. Available from: http://scenecreek.com/jonathan-narducci-talks-about-love-me/ [Accessed 15 Feb 2018].

Lacan, J., 2006. The Mirror Stage as Formative of the I Function as Revealed in Psychoanalytic Experience. In: *Écrits*. New York: W.W. Norton & Company.

Lee, V., 2016. Avi Mograbi won't give up on the viewers. *Haaretz* [online]. 23 June 2016. Available from: https://www.haaretz.co.il/blogs/veredlee/1.2984934 [Accessed 26 Jan 2018].

Leeman, L., 2003. How Close Is Too Close? A Consideration of the Filmmaker-Subject Relationship. *International Documentary*, 22 (5 (June)), 14–18.

Lenin, V. I., 1934. *Collected Works*. New York: International Publishers.

Leopold, D., 2013. Marxism and Ideology: From Marx to Althusser. In: *The Oxford Handbook of Political Ideologies*. Oxford: Oxford University Press.

Letort, D., 2014. Agnès Varda: filming the Black Panthers's Struggle. *L'Ordinaire des Amériques*, (217).

Lorber, F., 2017. Paukenschlag in Antisemitismus-Debatte. *FURIOS Online* [online]. 5 July 2017. Available from: http://www.furios-campus.de/2017/07/05/paukenschlag-in-antisemitismus-debatte/ [Accessed 10 Jan 2018].

Lotus Films, 2018. *Workingman's Death – Lotus-Film* [online]. Available from: http://www.lotus-film.at/filme/workingmans-death [Accessed 28 Mar 2018].

Love Me, 2017. *Love Me – The Documentary*. Love Me – The Documentary [online]. Available from: http://www.lovemethedocumentary.com/ [Accessed 14 Mar 2017].

Lukács, G., 1970. *Writer and Critic*. London: Merlin Press.

Lukács, G., 1971. *History and Class Consciousness, Studies in Marxist Dialectics*. London: Merlin Press.

Lukács, G., 1979. *The Meaning of Contemporary Realism*. London: Merlin Press.

MacArthur Foundation, 2018. About Us — *MacArthur Foundation* [online]. Available from: https://www.macfound.org/about/ [Accessed 15 Feb 2018].

MacDougall, D., 1995. Beyond Observational Cinema. *In*: Hockings, Paul, ed. *Principles of Visual Anthropology*. Berlin: Mouton de Gruyter, 115–132.

MacDougall, D., 1998. *Transcultural Cinema*. Princeton: Princeton University Press.

Magnolia Pictures, 2018. Man on Wire (Official Movie Site) –Starring Philippe Petit, Jean François Heckel and Jean-Louis Blondeau – Available on DVD – Trailer, Pictures & More [online]. Available from: http://www.magpictures.com/manonwire/ [Accessed 27 Mar 2018].

Marx, K. and De Leon, D., 1898. *The Eighteenth Brumaire of Louis Bonaparte*. New York: International Publishers.

Marx, K. and Engels, F., 1959. *Das Kapital, a Critique of Political Economy*. Chicago: H. Regnery.

Marx, K. and Engels, F., 1969. Die deutsche Ideologie. *In*: *Werke* [online]. Berlin: Dietz Verlag. Available from: http://www.mlwerke.de/me/me03/me03_009.htm [Accessed 1 Oct 2016].

Mauldin, B., 2014. Black Panthers. *Senses of Cinema* [online]. Available from: http://sensesofcinema.com/2014/cteq/black-panthers-2/ [Accessed 5 Feb 2018].

Mayhew, H., 1861. *London Labour and the London Poor*. England: Griffin, Bohn, and Company.

McLane, B. A., 2012. *A New History of Documentary Film*. New York: Continuum.

Miller, J., 2011. 24 Lies Per Second: an Auteurist Analysis of the Documentary Films of Errol Morris. *Digital Window @ Vassar* [online]. Available from: http://digitalwindow.vassar.edu/cgi/viewcontent.cgi?article=1157&context=senior_capstone [Accessed 18 Feb 2017].

Mooney, J., 2015. The Importance of Form: Introduction to Film Studies. *Filmosophy* [online]. Available from: https://filmandphilosophy.com/2015/01/29/the-importance-of-form-introduction-to-film-studies/ [Accessed 17 Oct 2017].

Moviemento, 2016. *Cinema Moviemento – Facebook Post* [online]. Available from: https://moviemento.de/AktuelleFilme/myland.

html?fbclid=IwAR1l7wfLocPb_FIpOzQH8R-K50Xd0ITZNa-vab4k4lus2ijpV2mg9Ia7pvw [Accessed 11 Dec 2019].

Mulvey, L., 1989. Visual Pleasure and Narrative Cinema. In: *Visual and Other Pleasures*. London: MacMillan Press, 6–18.

Myers, A., 2012. Interview with Steve Wiebe of 'The King of Kong: A Fistful of Quarters' (Part 1). *Mediascape Blog* [online]. Available from: http://www.tft.ucla.edu/mediascape/blog/interview-with-steve-wiebe-of-the-king-of-kong-a-fistful-of-quarters-part-1/ [Accessed 15 Feb 2018].

Naficy, H., 2007. Ethnography and African Culture: Jean Rouch on La Chasse au Lion à L'arc and Les maîtres fous. In: ten Brink, J., ed. *Building Bridges: The Cinema of Jean Rouch*. London: Wallflower.

Narducci, J., 2015. How Do You Document Love? The Making of Mail-Order Bride Documentary Love Me. *MovieMaker Magazine* [online]. Available from: https://www.moviemaker.com/archives/moviemaking/directing/document-love-making-mail-order-bride-documentary-love/ [Accessed 15 Feb 2018].

New Line Cinema, 2018. *The King of Kong: A Fistful of Quarters* [online]. Available from: https://web.archive.org/web/20120307231337/http://www.newline.com/properties/kingofkongtheafistfulofquarters.html [Accessed 11 Dec 2018].

NFCT, 2018. פעם נכנסתי לגן | *NFCT* [online]. Available from: http://nfct.org.il/blog/movies/%d7%a4%d7%a2%d7%9d-%d7%a0%d7%9b%d7%a0%d7%a1%d7%aa%d7%99-%d7%9c%d7%92%d7%9f9f/ [Accessed 27 Mar 2018].

Nicholas, J. and Price, J., 1998. *Advanced Studies in Media*. Cheltenham: Nelson Thomas.

Nichols, B., 1981. *Ideology and the Image: Social Representation in the Cinema and Other Media*. Bloomington: Indiana University Press.

Nichols, B., 1991. *Representing Reality: Issues and Concepts in Documentary*. Bloomington: Indiana University Press.

Nichols, B., 2006. What to Do About Documentary Distortion? Toward a Code of Ethics. *International Documentary Association* [online]. Available from: https://www.documentary.org/content/what-do-about-documentary-distortion-toward-code-ethics-0 [Accessed 10 Jan 2018].

Nichols, B., 2001. *Introduction to Documentary*. Bloomington: Indiana University Press.

Nichols, B., 2010. *Introduction to Documentary, Second Edition*. Bloomington: Indiana University Press.

Ofir, J., 2016. American Jewish Committee Agent Tries to Dig Up Anti-Semitic Dirt in a German Refugee Housing Block. *Mondoweiss* [online]. 28 January 2016. Available from: http://mondoweiss.net/2016/01/

american-jewish-committee-agent-tries-to-dig-up-anti-semitic-dirt-in-a-german-refugee-housing-block/ [Accessed 19 Feb 2017].

Ollman, B., 2003. *Dance of the Dialectic: Steps in Marx's Method*. Chicago: University of Illinois press.

PACBI, 2018. *PACBI-Israel's Exceptionalism: Normalizing the Abnormal* [online]. Available from: http://www.pacbi.org/etemplate.php?id=1749 [Accessed 23 Mar 2018].

Palumbo-Liu, D., 2015. Steven Salaita, Professor Fired for 'Uncivil' Tweets, Vindicated in Federal Court. *The Nation* [online]. 11 August 2015. Available from: https://www.thenation.com/article/steven-salaita-professor-fired-for-uncivil-tweets-vindicated-in-federal-court/ [Accessed 10 Jan 2018].

Patta, G., 2015. Exclusive Interview with Director Jonathon Narducci for 'Love Me' Documentary. *LRM Online* [online]. Available from: http://lrmonline.com/news/exclusive-interview-with-director-jonathon-narducci-for-love-me-documentary [Accessed 14 Mar 2017].

Piccirillo, R. A., 2011. The Technological Evolution of Filmmaking and Its Relation to Quality in Cinema. *Inquiries Journal/Student Pulse*, 3 (8), 1.

Prédal, R., 1982. Jean Rouch, un griot gaulois. *CinémAction*, 17, 77–78.

Rabiger, M. and Hurbis-Cherrier, M., 2013. *Directing. Film Techniques and Aesthetics*. 5th ed. New York: Focal Press.

Rabinowitz, P., 1994. *They Must Be Represented: The Politics of Documentary*. London: Verso.

Reddy, P., n.d. The Poesis of Mimesis in Les Maîtres Fous: Looking Back at the Conspiratorial Ethnography of Jean Rouch. *African Film Festival Inc* [online]. Available from: http://www.africanfilmny.org/2000/the-poesis-of-mimesis-in-les-maitres-fous-looking-back-at-the-conspiratorial-ethnography-of-jean-rouch/ [Accessed 5 Feb 2018].

Resha, D., 2015. *The cinema of Errol Morris*. Middletown: Wesleyan University Press.

Rose, M., 2017. Not Media About, But Media With: Co-creation for Activism. In: Aston, J., Gaudenzi, S., and Rose, M., eds. *i-docs: The Evolving Practice of Interactive Documentary*. London: Wallflower, 49–65.

Ruby, J., 1991. Speaking For, Speaking About, Speaking With, or Speaking Alongside—An Anthropological and Documentary Dilemma. *Visual Anthropology Review*, 7 (2), 50–67.

Said, E. W., 1978. *Orientalism*. New York: Pantheon Books.

S-, F.-, 2013. The shocking truth. *The Economist* [online]. 27 August 2013. Available from: https://www.economist.com/blogs/prospero/2013/08/rise-documentary-film [Accessed 26 Jan 2018].

Shiff, E., 2009. Documents and Sings. *Walla! Culture* [online]. 6 February 2009. Available from: https://e.walla.co.il/item/1430861 [Accessed 26 Jan 2018].

Sim, G., 2012. Said's Marxism: Orientalism's relationship to film studies and race. *Discourse*, 34 (2), 240–262.

Sorenson, I. E., 2015. Go crowdfound yourself: some unintended consequences of crowdfunding for documentary film and industry in the UK. *In: MoneyLab Reader: An Intervention in Digital Economy*. Amsterdam: Institute for Networked Cultures, 268–280.

Sperber, M., 1996. Hoop Dreams, Hollywood Dreams. *Jump Cut*, (40), 3–7.

Steinlein, S., 2014. Schriftliche Fragen für den Monat Juli 2014 Frage Nr. 7-316.

Stone, P., 2014. Steve James. *My First Shoot* [online]. 21 January 2014. Available from: http://www.myfirstshoot.com/interview/steve-james/ [Accessed 24 Mar 2018].

Stutterheim, K., 2015. *Handbuch angewandter Dramaturgie*. Frankfurt/M: Peter Lang.

Stutterheim, K., 2016. Documentary Film Production under Neo-Liberal Circumstances –A Genre in Change.

Stutterheim, K., 2018. Documentary Film about History, for the Future. *In*: Post, D., ed. *Franco's Settlers*. Berlin: Play Loud! Productions.

Summerhayes, C., 2004. Haunting Secrets: Tracey Moffat's beDevil. *In: Film Quarterly*. (58), 14–24.

Berkley, CA: University of California Press Journals.

The Filmlot, 2012. The Filmlot Interview: Seth Gordon – Director of 'The King of Kong'. *The Filmlot* [online]. Available from: https://web.archive.org/web/20120322222322/http:/thefilmlot.com/interviews/INTsgordon.php. [Accessed 15 Feb 2018].

The Numbers, 2018. *Man on Wire (2008) – Financial Information* [online]. Available from: https://www.the-numbers.com/movie/Man-on-Wire [Accessed 15 Feb 2018].

Tsai, M., 2015. 'Welcome to Leith,' about White Supremacists, May Be Year's Scariest Movie. *LA Times* [online]. 5 November 2015. Available from: http://www.latimes.com/entertainment/movies/la-et-mn-welcome-to-leith-review-20151106-story.html [Accessed 15 Feb 2018].

Underhill, S., 2013. *Complete List of Commercial Films Produced with Assistance from the Pentagon*. Academia.edu [online]. Available from: https://www.academia.edu/4460251/Complete_List_of_Commercial_Films_Produced_with_Assistance_from_the_Pentagon [Accessed 27 Apr 2019].

Waugh, T., 2011. Acting to Play Oneself: Performance in Documentary. In: *The Right to Play Oneself: Looking Back on Documentary Film*. Minneapolis, MN: University of Minnesota Press.

Wayne, M., 2001. *Political Film: The Dialectics of Third Cinema*. London: Pluto Press.

Wayne, M., 2003. *Marxism and Media Studies: Key Concepts and Contemporary Trends*. London: Pluto Press.

Wayne, M., 2005. *Understanding Film: Marxist Perspectives*. London: Pluto Press.

Welcome to Leith, 2018. *Welcome to Leith* [online]. Available from: http://www.welcometoleithfilm.com/ [Accessed 27 Mar 2018].

Wiehl, A., 2017. Documentary as Co-Creative Practice, from Challenge for Change to Highrise: Kat Cizek in Conversation with Mandy Rose. In: Aston, J., Gaudenzi, S., and Rose, M., eds., *i-docs: The Evolving Practice of Interactive Documentary*. London: Wallflower.

Williams, R., 2005. Base and Superstructure in Marxist Cultural Theory. In: *Culture and Materialism: Selected Essays*. London: Verso.

Winston, B., 2008. *Claiming the Real II: Documentary: Grierson and Beyond*. London: British Film Institute.

Wolff, M., 2018. *Fire and Fury: Inside the Trump White House*. London: Little, Brown.

Yehuda, L., Suciu, A., Palgi-Hecker, H., Bendel, M., and Jaraisy, R., 2014. *One Rule, Two Legal Systems: Israel's Regime of Laws in the West Bank*. Israel: The Association for Civil Rights in Israel.

Young, J. C., 2017. We Can't Keep Examining 'White Working Class' Voters Without Calling Out Their Racism. *Huffington Post* [online]. Available from: https://www.huffingtonpost.com/entry/we-cant-keep-examining-white-working-class-voters_us_5a037ce9e4b055de8d096a41.

YouTube, n.d., בין גדרות, במאי: אבי מוגרבי, כתוביות עברית *BEIN GDEROT, HEB SUBS* [online]. Available from: https://www.youtube.com/watch?v=opS2U1-uNoE [Accessed 27 Mar 2018].

Z32, 2018. *Z32 – Home* [online]. Available from: https://www.facebook.com/Z32-243600962331316/ [Accessed 27 Mar 2018].

Zeitz, J., 2017. Does the White Working Class Really Vote Against Its Own Interests? *POLITICO Magazine* [online]. 31 December 2017. Available from: https://www.politico.com/magazine/story/2017/12/31/trump-white-working-class-history-216200 [Accessed 15 Feb 2018].

Babelsberger Schriften zur Mediendramaturgie und -Ästhetik

Herausgegeben von Kerstin Stutterheim

Band 1 Kerstin Stutterheim / Silke Kaiser: Handbuch der Filmdramaturgie. Das Bauchgefühl und seine Ursachen. 2., überarbeitete und erweiterte Auflage. 2011.

Band 2 Kerstin Stutterheim (Hrsg.): Studien zum postmodernen Kino. David Lynchs *Inland Empire* und Bennett Millers *Capote*. 2011.

Band 3 Tore Vagn Lid: Gegenseitige Verfremdungen. Theater als kritischer Erfahrungsraum im Stoffwechsel zwischen Bühne und Musik. 2011.

Band 4 Kerstin Stutterheim: Handbuch Angewandter Dramaturgie. Vom Geheimnis des filmischen Erzählens. Film, TV und Games. 2015.

Medienästhetik und Mediennutzung. Media Production & Media Aesthetics

Herausgegeben von Kerstin Stutterheim und Martina Schuegraf

Band 5 Gerd Naumann: Filmsynchronisation in Deutschland bis 1955. 2016.

Band 6 Mahelia Hannemann: Accept Diversity! Accept Equality? Eine analytische Untersuchung des Anspruchs und der Realität von Gleichstellung in der Filmindustrie mit Hinblick auf die Funktion des internationalen Filmfestivals Berlinale. 2016.

Band 7 Franziska An der Gassen: Der Deutsche Erfolgsfilm. Determinanten erfolgreicher Kinofilme und Typisierung eines „Deutschen Geschmacks" im Kontext zuschauerrelevanter Kriterien der Filmauswahl. 2019.

Band 8 Dror Dayan: The Manifestations of Political Power Structures in Documentary Film. 2020.

www.peterlang.com